AMERICA STREET

A JOURNEY OF PERSONAL TRANSFORMATION ACROSS RACIAL LINES IN THE DEEP SOUTH

AMERICA STREET

A JOURNEY OF PERSONAL TRANSFORMATION ACROSS RACIAL LINES IN THE DEEP SOUTH

MATTHEW PRIDGEN

LIONHEARTS PRESS

Charleston, SC

AMERICA STREET

A JOURNEY OF PERSONAL TRANSFORMATION ACROSS RACIAL LINES IN THE DEEP SOUTH

Copyright © 2020 by Matthew Pridgen

PUBLISHED BY LIONHEARTS PRESS
507 Front St, Unit #573
Summerville, SC 29486
lionheartspress.com

All rights reserved. No part of this book may be used or reproduced in any manner whatsoever without written permission except in the case of brief quotations embodied in critical articles and reviews.

The names and identifying details of some characters in this book have been changed.

All Scripture quotations, unless otherwise noted, have been taken from The Holy Bible, English Standard Version® (ESV®), copyright © 2001 by Crossway, a publishing ministry of Good News Publishers. Used by permission. All rights reserved.

Scripture quotations marked (NIV) are taken from the Holy Bible, New International Version®, NIV®. Copyright © 1973, 1978, 1984, 2011 by Biblica, Inc.™ Used by permission of Zondervan. All rights reserved worldwide. www.zondervan.com The "NIV" and "New International Version" are trademarks registered in the United States Patent and Trademark Office by Biblica, Inc.™

Scripture quotations marked (NLT) are taken from the Holy Bible, New Living Translation, copyright ©1996, 2004, 2015 by Tyndale House Foundation. Used by permission of Tyndale House Publishers, Inc., Carol Stream, Illinois 60188. All rights reserved.

Scripture quotations marked MSG are taken from THE MESSAGE, copyright © 1993, 2002, 2018 by Eugene H. Peterson. Used by permission of NavPress. All rights reserved. Represented by Tyndale House Publishers, Inc.

ISBN 978-0-9854127-5-3

Printed in the United States of America
First Edition 2020

*To my mom,
for always showing me
unconditional love in action*

Prologue

SIXTY GOLD COINS. I held in my hands a small fortune packaged in a box so small that when it first arrived, I had to do a double take. I had never owned gold or any precious metal before in my life and did not realize what a punch the tiniest amount could pack. Contained in a box about the size of two decks of cards stacked on top of one another, the 60 metal discs weighed as much as a small dumbbell and felt like gravity could at any moment rob them from my hands.

I held on tightly for two reasons, the first being the natural weight of a small, heavy box. But there was another sort of weight which caused my grip to be fiercer than normal and my palms to sweat just the slightest bit. Not only did the 60 one-ounce American Gold Eagle coins weigh more than I expected and arrive in a package smaller than I expected, they contained enough purchasing power to keep my small family of five afloat for the next two years as long as we stayed diligent about our budgeting and spending. For an unpaid street minister living by faith and a trickle of income from his wife's handful of very small business ventures, this was an attractive prospect.

It's one thing to have that sort of wealth in a bank where someone else is responsible for keeping it safe and where it is insured against loss or theft, and it's another thing when you have it literally in your own hands and it is not insured and no one else even knows about it and whatever happens is on your own head. Of course at home we kept it in a small safe hidden in a discrete location.

But even then I found myself fighting against roaming thoughts of "what if" scenarios. What if someone breaks in and finds the safe or what if we have a tornado or a flood and we have to evacuate or what if a code-cracking squirrel gets in through the roof and decides that he wants to diversify his winter portfolio and add gold to his single-faceted acorn holdings. It's amazing how the imagination can run wild about money when you let it.

In reality, a small amount of gold held in a decent safe in a well hidden spot in an average-sized house at the end of a quiet street is not much of a security threat, particularly if no one in the world other than you and your wife know it's there. But carrying it around in a little cardboard box out in the open added a whole new set of variables that I deliberately chose not to think too much about.

I had already made the three and a half mile drive down the peninsula from my house to the St. Philip's Chapel on Church Street where the worship service which was my destination had already begun. I sat on a hard wooden pew with virtually no outside threats to consider. The only thing going through my mind as I gripped this tiny fortune in my hands was whether or not I would actually do what God had told me to do and give it away.

INTRODUCTION

"It was the best of times, it was the worst of times, it was the age of wisdom, it was the age of foolishness, it was the epoch of belief, it was the epoch of incredulity, it was the season of light, it was the season of darkness, it was the spring of hope, it was the winter of despair."

Charles Dickens, A Tale of Two Cities

THE LATE MORNING SUN glistened off the choppy waves of the Charleston Harbor as I looked out over Castle Pinckney and Fort Sumter from the boat ramp of the Carolina Yacht Club. I took a deep breath as the salty air flooded my nostrils, immediately giving me that feeling of home we all inherently long for. Born and raised on the South Carolina coast, salt water has always been a way of life and has played a major part in my story in more ways than one.

As was the predictable pattern for our family boat trips, we were running late trying to pack coolers and towel bags for the day ahead. My aunt and uncle who were leading the expedition hadn't even arrived yet, and to their defense, corralling passengers for a boat cruise can be a monumental task.

Being the first to arrive, I was fighting internally to cherish the moment and to avoid getting pulled into the boat trip preparation drama. I closed my eyes and allowed the sun to bathe my face in warmth as I got lost in a sweet moment of restful tranquility and excited anticipation.

Just as I was drifting off into carefree contemplation, my phone rang, and as tempted as I was to ignore it, I pulled my phone out of my pocket and glanced at the caller ID. The display showed the name of a friend who I had met some years prior through a homeless outreach in the inner city. I hesitated for a moment but answered the call, and despite a feeling of slight annoyance at having interrupted my moment, I greeted my friend with a warm hello.

After exchanging pleasantries, she went on to explain that she was having a washing machine delivered to her apartment and that she needed help moving it from the truck into her laundry room. She had already informed me about the washer some days earlier with excitement in her voice at the prospect of no longer having to walk to the Laundromat. She had a bum knee, and the trek was wearing on her.

I quickly assessed the situation and made a rough calculation of the probability that my family would leave the dock before I had a chance to return. I decided that the odds were pretty slim, so I hopped into my car and drove off toward the Harris Street projects in the heart of Charleston's Eastside neighborhood. Only two miles up the peninsula from the Yacht Club, the Eastside was an entirely different world.

Fortunately for me, the washing machine arrived before I did, and the unloading process took only a few minutes. A mutual friend had picked it up earlier in the day, and the two of us were able to haul it inside with little trouble. The apartment was small and dingy with very poor lighting, as was the case with every project apartment I had ever visited. Although it was a tight squeeze, we found a spot for the washing machine and carefully maneuvered it into place.

INTRODUCTION

My friend was palpably excited and invited us to stay, but I told her that I had to run, hoping I would not arrive back at the Yacht Club just in time to see my uncle's boat disappear over the horizon. I raced back to the dock biting my fingernails the whole way only to find that the boat wasn't even in the water yet. Over an hour after our original ETA, we began our cruise and set off toward Morris Island, which was the destination for our picnic.

Later that evening, once we all returned home and the sunburn set in, I pondered the day's events. I thought about the stark disparity of the world I had been brought up in, the world of the Carolina Yacht Club and my home South of Broad, and the world my friend had been raised in, the world of Section Eight housing and the constant struggle to buy pet food for her beloved cat, Sugarplum. I wondered how many others had ever made the same one-day road trip I had that morning, from the Carolina Yacht Club to the Eastside and back.

My heart in writing this book is to explore the two worlds I have unintentionally found myself living between on a daily basis. My life has become a tale of two cities, not London and Paris separated by border lines and hundreds of miles, but two cities in one, two completely foreign universes locked together within a common border on the small peninsula of Charleston, sometimes a couple of miles apart and other times right next door.

This book is a tale of black and white, rich and poor, the haves and the have-nots. And whether we like it or not, we all play a part in the drama. Our lives are all entwined into one common destiny, one shared future, one community with an interwoven narrative. We each have what the other needs, yet a wall as impenetrable as the palmetto logs of Fort Sumter has for four centuries stood between our two worlds—and between our hearts.

Chapter One

The Tent

"**Why did you** take my church down?"

The Charleston air hung heavy and hot all around us as Latoyah looked up at me with her big brown eyes and batted her eyelashes to complete the best sad puppy dog look I had ever seen. If there was a worldwide sad puppy dog face competition, and who knows maybe there is somewhere, this girl would easily take home first prize.

Two weeks ago, I had never seen Latoyah before in my life—not until she came skipping into the tent revival where I baptized her and seven of her friends, all between the ages of eight and ten. As she stood in front of me, I couldn't help but notice how pale and white my complexion appeared next to her obsidian skin. Contrast truly was the mark of our relationship.

Her question penetrated my heart. Everything in me wanted to put the tent back up, to give her what she wanted, to give her the whole world. But the tent revival was over, and I'm not sure I would have survived the wrath of my wife if I were to have told her that I was going out preaching even one more night and leaving her at home with our almost two-year-old son, our two-month-old twin boys, and her father who was almost completely crippled by advanced-stage Parkinson's.

Fourteen days in a row I preached under that tent, every night at 7:00 p.m., and rarely did I get home before 11:00. My wife and I both were ready to get back to life as normal, but not Latoyah. And not the other girls either. They had found God under that tent. A home. A place where they were unconditionally loved and accepted. A place where they could dance and sing and worship the Lord with abandon. They had been baptized under that tent, the tabernacle where they began their journey with Jesus Christ.

The 100 by 40 foot tent stood on the corner of Meeting and Lee Streets in downtown Charleston on the edge of the Eastside neighborhood where most of the city's project housing is located. Growing up, we always drove *around* the Eastside. In fact, I didn't even know that it existed. That poverty existed. I knew there were bad parts of town and that you locked your doors if you ever had to drive through. But for the most part, I was completely oblivious to the wealth divide, and to the depth of the racial divide, that still lingers to this day in nearly every city and town in the South.

As I stood with Latoyah right across the street from the project housing where she had lived her entire life, I could not help but feel the disparity. The row after row after row of squatty, dilapidated brick apartments made my family home look like a mansion. And by any other than American standards, it was a mansion, just three miles down the peninsula on the battery in the heart of Charleston' famous South of Broad neighborhood.

It would be impossible to count the number of times I had driven up and down the peninsula, right past the projects and right past Latoyah. I remember thinking that if I were to ever stop on America Street that I would probably get shot. I don't know where that thought even came from, but it was somehow cemented in my mind as an inevitability from childhood.

Now just yards away from the street that had become so infamous in my psyche growing up, what stood out was not some sort of threat to my safety, but rather the amount of litter swirling around my feet in the breeze and the deserted plainness of a neighborhood left behind and left out of the hustle and bustle and rapid development of the recently discovered Southern gem of a city that is Charleston, South Carolina.

Latoyah and I had almost nothing in common except for our humanity and the fact that life and God had somehow brought us together. The honest truth is that I did not hold a tent revival on the Eastside of downtown Charleston with little girls in mind. My heart was for the homeless and the poor, the oppressed and the marginalized, the drug addict and the alcoholic, the drug dealer and the gang banger, the struggling single mothers and grandmothers and even great grandmothers raising a generation while the fathers rotate in and out of a broken criminal justice system.

I will never forget driving up to an apartment complex in North Charleston with a friend and engaging in a conversation with a Black young man about nine or ten years old. We said hello and without any prompting, he asked if we were from the Department of Corrections. Two fairly light skinned guys (my friend is Hawaiian but jokes that everyone thinks he is Hispanic) show up at your front door and the first thing that crosses your mind is that somebody's going to jail.

It was the young Black men who my heart was broken for, yet it was eight little Black girls who showed up at the tent. But as Latoyah hugged me around the waist and looked up into my eyes, I knew there was a treasure here, one that I had overlooked and grossly undervalued my entire life.

I honestly had no idea what to do. What on earth did I know about elementary school girls? I was a street preacher who had spent the last decade of my life helping the homeless. Yet I knew that I had to do something. Of all the souls in all of Charleston, these were the ones God had decided to send my way. And if I know anything, I know the Lord loves every single one of his children the same.

These girls were infinitely precious in his sight and so I decided they would be in mine as well.

THE HILL

I STILL REMEMBER the first time I saw Hazel, sitting by herself on the far corner of the church property in Durham, North Carolina all the way across the parking lot from "the hill" where the rest of the homeless guys sat day after day on rickety, sun-bleached milk crates drinking 40s, smoking cigarettes and watching the world pass them by. I never noticed the small set of four or five brick stairs she was perched upon, or if I had, they had never jumped out at me, since all of my time, energy and focus were directed toward the guys at the other end of the parking lot.

I had graduated from Duke University two years prior and stayed in the area to take a job working for a small community development non-profit just down the road in Raleigh. Something about the church and the hill had captured my heart, and I chose the 25-mile commute from Durham to Raleigh rather than relocating into NC State territory.

Hazel sat with her arms folded across her knees almost in a fetal position staring out over the street corner where our sleepy, 100-year-old Episcopal church backed up to the service entrance of a Whole Foods grocery store whose employees would sometimes put out old produce for the homeless men. Captain John Bailey who ran security for the store would often come over to check on them and to offer a word of encouragement.

The Tent

Captain Bailey was among a handful of kind folks from the community who truly had a heart for the homeless. You could usually tell who was in it for themselves, serving to appease their own guilty conscience, versus those who were in it to see lives changed and transformed. I often wondered where I fell along this spectrum and hoped and prayed that it was somewhere in the latter category.

There were a few guys on the hill when I arrived at the church that day but none of them knew anything about the gray-haired stranger sitting across the way. All I knew was that she looked like she could use a friend, so I mustered up some courage and began the short trek across the parking lot. I made a concerted effort to approach her as gently as possible, quietly yet firmly announcing my presence as I drew near to avoid startling her.

She turned her head casually to see who was walking up behind her, and upon seeing me, she acknowledged my presence with a small almost imperceptible movement of her head. Her hair was matted and tangled, and her oversized plaid shirt hung from her body so loosely that it looked like a small tent flowing down from her neck.

I took a seat on the ground next to her and introduced myself in an overly gregarious way, as was my custom, to put her at ease. I could feel the sadness emanating from her very being. It seemed to ooze from every pore and every breath and every word she uttered.

I found out that her name was Hazel, and as I began to ask about her situation, my suspicions were quickly confirmed. Hazel had been evicted from the apartment where she had spent the last 10 years, most recently working as a clerk at the Whole Foods across the street. She had been banned from the Whole Foods property due to her loitering after losing her job there some several months prior and now the economics of the situation had finally caught up to her.

She had nowhere to go and not even so much as an extra change of clothes, so she came to the most familiar place she knew, or at least as close as she could get to that familiar place, and there she sat—waiting, watching, thinking and processing this new curveball life had thrown her way.

The reason for my presence at the church that particular evening was to attend evening prayer, so after hearing Hazel's quandary, I invited her to join me inside the church, something I did with all of the homeless folks who showed up on our church property. Although I could count on one hand the number of times my offer was accepted, that did not stop me from extending the invitation again and again.

The little stone church, located just off of Duke University's east campus in the heart of Durham, had recently been through a dramatic split and left with no minister, no organist and about 20 faithful parishioners. Since there was no clergy or anyone working at the church during the week to run them off, the homeless guys had pretty much free reign of the dusty corner of the parking lot we all called the hill.

In order to avoid running into them, most of the folks who attended the church parked on a side street and walked to the sanctuary along the opposite side, and I was tempted to do the same. My concern with the guys was not so much about safety, but just that I tend to run right on time and our conversations often made me late for church, a major faux pas in the South. Plus, you never know when you will be put in the uncomfortable position of someone asking you for something that you're not so thrilled to give away.

But late or not and uncomfortable or not, I decided that I would at very least give them the time of day and made a commitment to myself to park in the very first spot right next to the hill every time I drove to the church for any reason. My conversations with the guys grew longer and longer, and I began making arrangements to arrive

10 or 15 minutes early to make sure that I had enough time to catch up with everyone. I went from standing over the crates to having one of my very own, and on the weekends and in my free time, I would often go and just sit with the guys on the hill.

Before I sat down, the guys would always search for a nice milk crate, one that didn't have any cracks on the top, and bring it over to me. I didn't like them making a fuss over me, so one time I quickly sat on one of the broken crates before they could get up, and after promptly falling straight through, I never again took their kindness for granted.

As I sat with the guys, I listened to the stories of how these men ended up spending most of their days and nights in the parking lot of a sleepy, old church. The more I listened and the more stories I heard, the more God began to change the way I viewed and interacted with them.

I remember Kenny who had been convicted of second degree murder more than two decades prior to our meeting. He claimed it was self defense, but the charge stood and he served 17 years in a Federal penitentiary. He told me that he had two options when applying for jobs. When asked if he had a criminal record, he could check "no" and get a job for two weeks or so, until the background check came back with a murder conviction on it. Or he could check "yes" and not get a job at all.

Kenny received partial disability for an injury he sustained while serving in the army, but it was not enough to rent a place—just enough to sustain a nasty alcohol and drug habit. So he spent most of his days on the hill drinking 40s and Wild Irish Rose, giving names to all of the squirrels and shooting the breeze with the other guys.

Then there was Brent. Brent had been committed for paranoid schizophrenia more times than anyone could count, and since there was no longer any place to take the mentally ill following the closure of Dorothy Dix hospital in Raleigh, the police would always just take him to the emergency room. There he would be admitted and medicated for a few days and then released with a month supply of Klonopin, which he ate like candy until he got high enough to pass out somewhere. When he was sober, Brent was one of the sweetest and most gentle guys on the hill.

I discovered that none of these men were there by choice, that each one was a prisoner wearing chains of injury and illness, drug and alcohol addiction, criminal records, debt, trauma and abuse of all kinds. Some had aged out of the foster system, some were veterans, and many had debilitating conditions (both physical and mental) that prevented them from procuring steady employment. I stopped seeing homeless men and starting seeing broken children of God, my very own brothers.

I could relate to these guys. I had been so broken by my failed drug-induced suicide attempt the summer before I stumbled upon the hill that I hardly knew how to engage with people anymore. In a way, I felt more comfortable with the homeless than I did with my best friends who were my roommates at Duke and who all went on to become doctors and lawyers and investment bankers.

I initially went to the church looking for God, but instead found him right there in the parking lot. I stumbled upon the hill quite by accident and realized that these guys and I shared a common thread—we were all broken. I began sharing my story with the homeless men who frequented the hill and got a totally different reception than I did from my college friends who didn't want to hear a word of it.

I heard an illustration one time that stuck. Imagine breaking a cookie in two, right down the middle. Now picture placing the two halves next to each other on a plate and fitting them together until the crack is no longer visible. Someone might look at the cookie on the plate and think that it is one whole cookie, but it's not. The cookie is broken and it will never be completely whole again despite how it appears.

This is exactly how I felt after my encounter in the ocean, like I had been broken in two and put back together again. And I knew that at any moment, the crack running right down the middle of my core might be exposed. All of a sudden, I felt more comfortable with these homeless guys than I did with my closest friends who I had lived with for three years. The guys on the hill were broken just like me, and they knew it—and we weren't trying to hide the crack any more.

The Fast That I Choose

As I walked through the doors of the church, I felt a wave of sadness wash over me as I thought about Hazel's situation. I normally enjoyed evening prayer—the sparseness of the plain wooden interior of the church, the simple and repetitive nature of the canticles, the scripture readings and the prayers—but on this particular night, I could not get my mind off of her. She was the first homeless female I had ever met on the hill.

A single scripture kept coming to mind that was not part of the daily readings, but it was one that had stuck with me ever since I read it due to its shocking relevance (despite having been written more than 2,500 years ago):

"Is not this the fast that I choose: to loose the bonds of wickedness, to undo the straps of the yoke, to let the oppressed go free, and to break every yoke? Is it not to share your bread with the hungry and bring the homeless poor into your house; when you see the naked, to cover him, and not to hide yourself from your own flesh?

Then shall your light break forth like the dawn, and your healing shall spring up speedily; your righteousness shall go before you; the glory of the LORD shall be your rear guard" (Isaiah 58:6-8).

Isaiah is addressing the spiritual leaders of his day and directly confronting their lifestyle of offering regular penance to God. He is reminding them of God's priority system, that while fasting and prayer and daily devotion to the Lord are all good things, at the end of the day if they do not lead us to a lifestyle of love and mercy, then they are all for naught.

Here I was praying the daily office to the Lord in a beautiful century-old church with stained glass windows that would knock your socks off and there sat a homeless woman on the edge of the property with nowhere to go. My mind started racing. I had an extra bedroom in my apartment just a quarter of a mile away which I had furnished for this exact purpose. The Word of God continued to penetrate my heart. "Is it not to share your bread with the hungry and bring the homeless poor into your house?"

I left the service that night with a heavy heart and a weight on my conscience like I had never felt before. It was one thing for guys to sleep on the hill, but I knew it was no place for a woman. I spoke to Hazel again on the way to my car, and since she did not ask me for anything, I justified my leaving. I drove home that night and tried to get her off my mind, but my efforts proved completely futile. The lingering conviction only got worse and worse, and I knew there was no escaping it.

I had heard all of the horror stories about people who opened their houses to the homeless only to be robbed or hurt or worse. But at the same time, I knew from firsthand experience that the homeless are much more likely to be victims of violence than perpetrators of it. I recognized that there was certainly a major risk of bringing a stranger into my home, but at the same time, I did not sense any sort of threat from my initial visit with Hazel. What I sensed more than anything was the immensity of her brokenness and the immediacy of her need.

As I prayed over the situation, I could see a very light rain beginning to fall, almost like a mist, outside of my apartment window. I trudged back out to my car and began the short drive to the church. I drove much slower than normal and paused for an unusually extended amount of time, even for a polite southerner, at all of the stop signs along the way. When I finally pulled into the parking lot, I looked around and breathed a sigh of relief. Hazel was nowhere in sight.

I had not articulated this as a prayer, but it was sort of a secret hope that perhaps the Lord was just testing me to see if I would be faithful and respond to the prompting that he had laid on my heart, only to arrive and discover that it was all a test. I sat in the parking lot for a few moments and looked around to be sure that she was no longer around. I felt a tremendous weight lifted off of my shoulders and lifted my foot from the brake to head back to my apartment.

At that very moment, Hazel appeared from around the side of the church walking with Concrete, our resident homeless ambassador. He was likely showing her around the place and pointing out the Tupperware bins where the church had arranged for the homeless residents to store their belongings. My heart sank for just a moment, but I quickly reminded myself that this was the purpose of my trip and thanked Jesus for the opportunity to be his hands and his feet.

I stepped out of the car into the misting rain and waved to Hazel and Concrete. They walked over to my car, and I extended an offer for her to stay at my place for the night. I had invited Concrete to stay before but he always refused to even come inside, either my apartment or the church, so I knew he would not feel excluded. Without saying a word, Concrete extended his arm and opened his hand, gesturing to Hazel to take me up on my offer, and after only a slight moment of hesitation, Hazel got into the passenger side door and off we drove back home.

A New Chapter

When we arrived at my apartment, I showed Hazel the guest bedroom where she would be staying and offered to wash her clothes for her while she took a shower. Her clothes stunk to high heaven, and I knew it had been a while since she had been able to bathe. Since she literally only had the clothes on her back, I gave her my smallest pair of basketball shorts and a t-shirt to wear while we waited for her clothes to be washed and dried.

Being six foot six, my shorts reached all the way down to her ankles and my shirt could have been a nightgown. We both had a good laugh about her new evening attire. I made some quick dinner for us, and we sat down at the table together while I listened to her story.

Hazel had been successful in her youth, always finding and keeping a job, but as she had gotten older and grayer, the service industry had closed off to her more and more until it became a real struggle to find steady employment. After losing her job at Whole Foods, she was not able to find anything else and got so behind on her rent that her landlord evicted her and padlocked her front door.

As she spoke, her eyes remained glued to the floor and she rarely even glanced up. Occasionally, she would crack a joke and her eyes would dart up to meet mine for a brief moment before she shifted her gaze back downward. Although I was able to hear most of her story, I had to strain my ears and even then there were parts that I missed due to her simple lack of volume. But I did not interrupt as there is something special about being heard and sharing your life's journey with a fellow traveler who takes an interest.

I have been convinced for a long time now that one of the greatest gifts anyone can give to the homeless is that of a listening ear. Many people talk to the homeless and give them a dollar here or a meal there, but very few take the time to actually listen. Mostly it seems, the ones who listen to the homeless are homeless themselves. I have sat with many a homeless man or woman on the side of the road or on the edge of a sidewalk and experienced the total neglect they feel as they are driven past, stepped over and overlooked.

As I listened to Hazel speak, I wondered if I had ever met a more gentle and timid soul in my life. I began to laugh at myself immediately when we got into my apartment for allowing fear to grip me so strongly earlier as I stood next to this woman who could not have been an inch more than five feet tall and who weighed maybe 90 pounds on a good day.

Her occasional grin gave me a glimpse of a jagged snarl tooth that, combined with her scraggly, thinning gray hair, gave her the appearance of a cartoon witch. I thought that if you were to encounter her in a dark alleyway, it would really put a pep in your step to keep moving along. But here in the light of my apartment, sitting at my small breakfast table, I felt that she was perhaps the most harmless human being who had ever walked the Earth.

That's how it often is with the homeless. The imagined or perceived threat of danger is so far from the reality of the situation in most cases that it's laughable—that is, if it weren't so tragic. I have met violent homeless individuals on rare occasion, but have found they comprise the vast minority of those who live on the streets. From my experience, most homeless people are so fraught with fear and pain and worry about their situation that they don't have any energy left over to be much of a threat to anyone.

It's hard to read scripture and miss God's heart for the poor. They say that there is no such thing as minor surgery when you are the one going under the knife. It's the same with the poor and the homeless. It's easy to call it a minor thing or to ignore it when it's happening to someone else. But when you are the one who is completely destitute, without a place to lay your head for the night, without food to eat, without an extra pair of clothes, or without a friend or family member to call, it's a much different story. Pain is real, and we as Christians do not have the moral right to ignore it.

The biggest problem we have with the homeless is that we tend to judge the negative behaviors that we observe on the surface rather than seeking to understand the root of those behaviors. We see a homeless man with a beer and assume that alcoholism is his main problem and the reason for his homelessness. We imagine that if he could only kick the bottle, he would be able to get back on his feet. What we don't take into consideration is the years of abuse that he suffered as a child that drove him to alcohol to numb the pain.

As Hazel continued to share her past, I knew in my spirit that there was something more, a missing link that connected her vibrant past to her broken present. And sure enough, she went on to share how she had been walking across Duke University's East campus one night, when she was attacked and raped by a complete stranger. The assault and violation of her person had impacted her profoundly and had sent her into a downward spiral of depression and isolation that marked her life moving forward.

Over time, Hazel became a complete recluse and an alcoholic, keeping to herself to avoid being hurt again and drinking to numb her painful past. The Hazel that sat across from me that night was only the shell of her former self. We often look at brokenness at this extreme level and immediately run in the other direction to avoid having to deal with it. We blame people for their broken behaviors and don't take the time to consider how or why these things came about. But the reality is that Hazel's brokenness arose out of a place of such intense hurt and pain that she can hardly be blamed for the outcome.

Jesus began his public ministry by quoting from Isaiah 61, "The Spirit of the Lord God is upon me because the Lord has anointed me to bring good news to the poor." The word for poor used here means physically poor (which Hazel was with only the clothes on her back) but it also means humble, afflicted and meek, depressed in mind or circumstances. There is something about the rock bottom moments in our lives that open us up to receiving the good news.

If there was one thing I realized as I sat there listening to Hazel share her story, it was the fundamental truth that although our life circumstances were totally different, at the core, we were both the same. I know that I was far too proud to receive the good news before I ended up at the brink of death in the middle of the ocean. God could have sent me the best preacher in the world, and his words would have fallen on deaf ears. But after the hard shell of my pride and the delusion of self-sufficiency were broken off of my life, then and only then was I prepared to hear what God had to say to me.

Hazel was and is a beautiful soul. And all of the pain and all of the affliction she had experienced was now coming together to provide a platform for the good news like never before. I told her how much God loved her and reassured her that it was not her fault for what happened to her. Jesus said that the enemy comes to steal and kill and destroy. Satan stole something from her that was so precious that it almost destroyed her life. But, as I reminded her, God still has a plan and a purpose even for her even in the midst of pain and suffering, and that He would use all of it for good.

After more than an hour, we both retired to our respective rooms and I instinctively locked the door to my bedroom. Better safe than sorry, I thought. I laid down in my bed and marveled at how peaceful I felt. Just a few hours before, I had had so much anxiety in my chest that I thought I might die. But now that I had been obedient to the prompting in my spirit and more importantly now that Hazel was safe and dry, an overwhelming sense of rest and calm came over me.

I felt somehow that I was beginning a new chapter in my walk with God, but I knew that he would be faithful to walk me through it. I walked over to the door and twisted the small lock to the unlocked position and began to get ready for bed.

Concrete

"**How can you** take someone into your house one day and leave them out in the streets the next?"

Concrete looked at me intently for just a moment and then burst into a chuckle, slapping me on the arm with the back of his hand. It was the Sunday morning after I had taken Hazel into my apartment two nights prior. She stayed with me on Friday night and then I dropped her off at the church on Saturday morning before heading to Raleigh for the day, which was 25 miles up the road. By the time I got back Saturday evening, Hazel was nowhere to be found.

Concrete was a complete enigma to me and to everyone else on the hill. He had been homeless longer than any of the other guys and the best estimate anyone could ever give me was that he had spent 20 or 25 years on the street. No one knew anything about Concrete's past except Willie who had a family connection somewhere down the line. He told me the story about how Concrete's son had been murdered and had died in his father's arms. It was that event, according to Willie, that began his downward spiral to chronic homelessness.

The Tent

Concrete had a language of his own. He spoke in poetic riddles and ancient mysteries and I would often write down his Concrete-isms in hopes of cracking the code and deciphering the message. On occasion, Concrete would say something totally coherent and then I would always perk my ears. One time, I took him with me to get some fried chicken and he told me to buy enough for eight. When we had left the hill, there was only one other guy there, but it was Concrete, so I listened. When we returned, there were exactly eight guys on the hill to share in our feast.

Concrete's words penetrated my heart. I had been thinking about Hazel all day and all night since I dropped her off back at the church. I had originally planned just to give her a place to stay for one night to get her out of the rain and to give her a chance to wash her clothes and take a shower. But as I drove to Raleigh and back, I wondered if I had done the right thing by putting her back out on the street with nowhere to go.

I asked Concrete if he knew where Hazel was or where she had stayed the night, but he went right back to being good 'ole Concrete and told me something completely unrelated like how I should get a shirt with all of the flags of the world on it. I sat marveling at the Lord who always found a way to speak to me through even the most unlikely mediums, just as he spoke to Balaam through a donkey. I wondered if it was because Concrete's mind was so far gone that God could use him to deliver a timely word with no resistance. Either way, I knew it was the voice of Jesus, and more importantly the heart of Jesus, so I began to look for Hazel.

Jesus told a parable in the 25th chapter of Matthew about the Final Judgment and how God is going to sort people into two categories, which he describes as sheep and goats. To the sheep, he recounts how he had been hungry and thirsty and how they had given him food and drink, and how he had been naked and homeless and how they had clothed him and taken him in, and how he had been sick and in prison and how they had visited him. The sheep are shocked and ask when they had seen Jesus in any of these situations, to which he replies that whatever they did for the least, they did for him.

He goes on to address the goats in an equal and opposite manner and shares how he had been hungry and thirsty and how they had not given him food and drink, how he had been naked and homeless and how they had not clothed him and taken him in, and how he had been sick and in prison and how they had not visited him. The goats are perhaps even more shocked than the sheep for the revelation that they had denied the Creator of the Universe simple mercy and kindness, and they ask when they could have possibly ignored God himself. Whatever they did not do for the least, Jesus replies, they did not do for him.

I grew up in a Country Club neighborhood and did not know a single poor person that I can remember aside from the maid who cleaned our house once or twice a week (and at the time I didn't even know she was poor). I went to church every Sunday throughout my entire childhood, and all I remember is doodling on the program and counting down the minutes until the service was over. I can't recount a single time I encountered Jesus Christ in a church building. But I met him on the streets. Time and time again, I have encountered God face to face among the homeless, the poor and the broken, and it has changed me to the core.

I knew as soon as Concrete spoke the words that it was God speaking to me. Although my plan was to help a lady get out of the rain for a night, God's plan was to give her a fresh start. I resigned in my heart to do God's will and to bring Hazel into my home with no deadline other than her finding her next step in life. I counted the cost as Jesus had instructed his own disciples and I prepared my heart for a journey into the unfamiliar.

The Tent

I was not able to find Hazel that morning, so I took a ride back over to the church in the early evening. I pulled up to the church to find Hazel and Concrete on the hill sitting on milk crates with a couple of the guys. I guess they had welcomed her into the fold, and she looked like she fit right in with her lumberjack-sized plaid shirt and faded blue jeans. I was glad to see she wasn't sitting all alone on the steps anymore.

I hopped out of the car, greeted the guys quickly and asked if she wanted to stay another night. She responded with a nod and a smile, and we were off. I didn't want to upset any of the other guys by showing favoritism to one over another, but we all knew that the hill was no place for a woman and I didn't get too much grief from the rest of the group.

This time I gave Hazel a key so she could come and go while I was at work, and I laid down a couple of ground rules. I told her that I had to go to work in the morning but that I would be back in the evening and that we could have dinner and make a plan for her. She also needed clothes and well, everything else, so we planned a trip to Walmart and the thrift store. Then she shared the real desire of her heart, which was to get her belongings out of her old apartment that was still padlocked.

After a quick dinner and a long shower, Hazel retired to her room and closed the door. I felt a nervous excitement about all that had just transpired. I had actually rented this apartment just a quarter mile from the church with the thought of having one or two of the guys come to live with me. Yet suddenly God had made the first move on my behalf, and here I was thrust into what felt like a whole new level of commitment to homeless ministry.

Although I certainly felt a mixture of emotions, one thing stood out to me above them all. I felt an overwhelming sense of peace. I knew that this new housing arrangement was orchestrated by God and I had simply obeyed his voice. I can count on one hand the number of times Concrete spoke to me directly and coherently the way he did that Sunday morning. God had used him to catapult me past my fears into a compassionate response to a desperate situation.

With Hazel and her 90 pound frame, my fear was not physical harm, and since I didn't really own anything of value or that was not replaceable, theft was not a major concern. What I feared, if I had to be completely honest, was the indefiniteness of her stay. She had no resources, no job prospects, not even any clothes or hygiene supplies. She was past her prime as far as the service industry is concerned—her hair was gray and beyond scraggly plus she had a mean snarl tooth. How on earth was she going to get a job?

But in that moment, I knew God had a plan. And whether she stayed with me for three days or three years, I surrendered it completely to Jesus. Because according to his own parable, he was the one staying under my roof. And there was no greater honor I could think of in all the world.

A Grueling Trek

A FEW DAYS AFTER Hazel moved in the second time, we received a glimmer of hope from a friend of mine who worked in full-time homeless ministry. There was a facility in Raleigh for women with drug and alcohol addiction that Hazel might qualify for. We set up a meeting in the late evening the following day and met at one of the picnic tables on the far end of the church property.

During the meeting, Hazel admitted her alcohol addiction and how it had been a major catalyst of her downward spiral. She mentioned some of the trauma she had been through in her life and shared even more than she had several nights before at my kitchen table. Having a female confidant allowed her to open up, and after many tears shed on both sides, Hazel agreed to receive help and got into the car to head straight over to the rehab facility.

Once the car had pulled away, I felt a major relief come over me and a weight lifted from my shoulders. I had just been wrestling with the possibility of a long-term stay for Hazel, but now she had been whisked away to a place that sounded like it could be the gateway to healing and restoration for her. I thanked God for providing for Hazel so swiftly and so decisively, and I returned home to get some rest.

The next three days were uneventful as I went back and forth, as was my routine, past the hill to evening prayer at the church. Then on the fourth day after Hazel left for the recovery house, I received a shock when I pulled up to the church. There was Hazel sitting on a milk crate with the guys on the hill. I didn't want to show my disappointment that she had left the program so soon, so I gained my composure and approached the hill, claiming a milk crate of my own right next to Hazel.

As I began to question her about her time, she immediately started talking about her stuff that was still in the apartment. She explained how she had liked the facility but that she had to get her stuff before she could ever stay for the long haul. She began listing all of the different valuables and keepsakes that were locked up in the apartment she had been evicted from.

I asked her if she would be willing to stay in the program if I was able to take care of retrieving her stuff. She sounded excited about this prospect and fished out of her pocket a card with her former landlord's phone number on it. I told her that I would call the next day and see if I could set up a meeting to get her belongings out of the apartment. She gave me a list of what to look for and I took notes on my phone.

I then called the social worker back and informed her of Hazel's departure from the facility. She said that Hazel would be eligible to go back but that she would have to really want it. I explained the situation with her belongings and how I was going to work on that to give Hazel peace of mind. She seemed satisfied and agreed to meet us at the church.

As we waited, I asked Hazel how she had gotten back to Durham, which was a good 25 miles away from Raleigh, assuming that she had hitched a ride with someone only discover that she had walked along the side of I-40 the entire way. I could not imagine how grueling that 25-mile trek must have been on foot in the North Carolina heat with no shade.

The nonprofit worker showed up just a few minutes later and after a second interview (which sounded more like a personal coaching session), Hazel was whisked away once again to the rehab facility. Somehow during her epic journey, she had landed some booze, which meant that she would have to go through detox again, but Hazel agreed as long as I promised to get her stuff out for her. I was more than willing and only wanted to see Hazel get set free from the alcohol addiction that had plagued her for so long.

The Charmer

"**Put this on.**"

One of the two Mexican workers who the landlord had sent to meet us at Hazel's apartment handed me a facemask before putting one over his own nose and mouth. I paused for a moment with the mask in my hand and looked at him inquisitively. He pointed to his friend who was wearing a mask and then back to me, gesturing adamantly that I put it on.

The Tent

The front door was nailed shut so he led us around back. On the way, we passed a huge dead rat lying just a foot from the foundation of the house. The hair on the back of my neck began to stand on end in anticipation of what I was about to see. But nothing could have prepared me for it.

The second worker approached the back door, put the key in and turned the knob. The door did not budge initially so he threw his whole body weight into it led by his right hip and jarred it open about three feet. He then stood back, extended his arm and opened his hand to give me the go ahead. I looked back and forth between the two guys who were both waiting for me to make the next move.

As I approached the door, I could already see through the opening the reason why the two men had insisted that I wear a facemask. A mountain of trash unlike any I had ever seen was piled against the back door preventing it from opening fully. I had to step up onto the trash heap to even enter the apartment.

It took my eyes a moment to adjust to the dimly lit room, so I stood for a few moments and prayed quietly to myself. As my vision began to come online, the silhouettes slowly became distinguishable and I could hardly believe what my eyes were seeing. The floor of the apartment was covered in two to three feet of trash that was piled up literally from wall to wall. Flattened out beer boxes lined the top of the mound to provide a walking path from one end to the other.

Peeking out from the endless expanse of garbage, I could see the top of the stove with its hood vent, a bookshelf full of dusty books and albums, and an empty coat rack all like mountain peaks emerging out of a dense fog of refuse. I began to recall Hazel's instructions of what to look for—her dresses, her books and her records—and how emphatic she had been in describing all of the valuable things she hoped to recover.

I stood for a moment completely stunned. I did not want to

disappoint Hazel, but I knew that there was nothing salvageable in this place. I found out from the landlord when I had talked to him on the phone that Hazel had lived there for several months without running water or electricity before he had been able to evict her. And apparently the rat on the side of the house was not alone.

    I slowly and carefully backed out of the door and removed my face mask. I walked around to the front of the house in a daze where the two men were on the porch working. I did not have many words, so I just waved and thanked them for their help. I climbed back into my car and took a deep breath. Now I understood what Kenny meant when he told me Hazel was a charmer, or someone who picks up anything that strikes their fancy. Over the course of 10 years, she had collected so many trifles and knick knacks that they overtook her. What she had convinced herself was a mountain of valuable treasure was actually a breeding ground for rodents and disease.

    I pulled out my cell phone to dial the landlord, and after several rings, I left a message that I was all done in the apartment and that I had not been able to salvage anything. I am beyond sure that he already knew this, but I was thankful that he let me figure it out for myself. As I began to drive off, I could see the two men working to get the front door open. I guess they were slated to tackle trash mountain, and boy did they ever have their work cut out for them. They could have filled two industrial dumpsters with all the garbage that was in that house. I did not envy the work that lay ahead for them.

One of the Girls

I did not want to break the bad news to Hazel about her belongings, but I also did not want to keep her waiting in anticipation. I called the social worker who had taken her to the rehab house in Raleigh twice now, and explained the situation. Before I could even finish, she told me that Hazel had once again left the facility. My heart sank. I had high hopes that this would be a place of real turnaround for Hazel and now after two misfires, the chances were slim of her ever sticking at a place like this.

Hazel showed back up at the hill about a day later. Since I had been given forewarning, there was no element of surprise, but I could not hide the sadness I felt over the situation. I gave Hazel a lift back to my apartment to regroup, and she began to tell me about her time in Raleigh. She said that the facility was nice and that she loved detox because she was totally alone for three days and could read all the books she wanted, but when they transferred her to the dorm where all of the other women stayed, she could not handle it. For a woman who had lived alone for 10 years, cohabitating with 20 other women in close quarters was a shock to the system. So she left, and as I feared, once again walked the 25 miles along the highway back to Durham.

I asked her what her plan was, and she shared her intention to get a job and eventually get back out on her own. We came up with a plan for her to visit two restaurants a day since the bulk of her work experience was in the food and beverage industry. We went to Walmart and the thrift store like we had planned and bought her clothes, hygiene supplies and a prepaid cell phone so she would have a phone number for her job applications.

A few weeks into her job search, I drove home to visit my folks in Charleston. I was not sure what to do with Hazel, but she had no other place to go and I had already been warned once before by the Lord about putting her out, so I told her to keep an eye on the place and headed home for the weekend.

On that following Sunday, my dad was not feeling well, so I took him to the emergency room where we found out the devastating news that he had an inoperable brain tumor. I called my work the next day and told them that I was not coming home. I called Hazel and let her know as well. I ended up staying at home for two weeks before I went back to Durham to begin packing up. My father was not going to be getting better and I knew that I needed to be home with him and to help my mom care for him in his last days.

When I arrived at my apartment in Durham, Hazel was sitting at the kitchen table where we had talked for the first time several weeks before. She was working on a crossword puzzle that looked like the ones my dad used to do with lots of blanks and 10 cent words that are too big and fancy to use in a real sentence and really only exist to show people how smart you are.

I had purchased two books of crossword puzzles for Hazel before I left and was amazed to find nearly every single puzzle finished with the exception of maybe a few blanks on each. I asked her if she used the answers in the back and she scoffed at me. This was one smart lady and I had to give credit where credit was due.

I told Hazel just a little bit about my trip and about the situation at home with my father and then I asked her how her job hunt was coming along. She looked at me and then down at the floor.

"I'm ready," she said gently.

It took me a moment to track with her. Ready for what? Then it hit me. She went on to explain how she had put in applications at every restaurant in town and that she had finally realized she was not as young as she used to be. She also realized that she had a real drinking problem and that she was ready to get real help.

As she shared, I could feel a change in her countenance, a true humility that did not exist before. She had lost everything she owned and now she had come face to face with the reality of her aging body and her uncontrollable urge to drink. Somewhere in the last two weeks, Hazel had hit rock bottom and her metamorphosis was palpable.

When Jesus gave his famous Sermon on the Mount, he opened with this cryptic statement, "Blessed are the poor in spirit, for theirs is the kingdom of God" (Matthew 5:3). The Message translation puts it like this: "You're blessed when you are at the end of your rope. With less of you, there is more of God and his rule." Even though she had walked out two times already, I knew in my heart that if she could get back to that place of recovery, she would stick it out this time.

I reached back out to the social worker who had helped us both times before. Amazingly, she was open to the idea and told me that Hazel could come back as many times as she liked. This woman truly had a heart for women and for people, and we set up one last appointment to meet with Hazel to get her back into the recovery program.

Two months later, I was back in Durham with my father getting treatments at Duke University Medical Center for his brain tumor and I swung over to Raleigh to check on Hazel. Since I was not allowed to go inside, she came out to the parking lot and greeted me. She told me that she was really liking the program and getting along with the other women much better than before. She had no more anchors holding her back, and she was beginning to move forward into her destiny unhindered.

I called around Hazel's six month mark just to check on her one last time. The lady on the phone told me that she could not disclose information about any of the women, but she remembered me from my visit and said, "Oh Ms. Hazel, she's just one of the girls."

I never saw or heard from Hazel again, but I know that she is in God's hands and that she has a fresh start towards a better life. I hope and pray that the Lord uses her as an instrument of healing for many others who have been violated and broken by the world and that her story will reach those who my story could never reach.

At the time, opening my home to Hazel seemed like the biggest leap of faith I had ever taken in my life, but now on the other side of it all, it seemed so normal. Why wouldn't I share my extra bedroom with someone in need? Why wouldn't I give her a key and let her come and go as she needed? She was an adult and a very smart one at that. In the end, the sacrifice I made seemed so insignificant in light of the outcome. I hardly did anything, but God took my small temporal sacrifice and made it into something eternal.

Jesus said not to store up treasure on earth, but to store up treasure in heaven. Hazel was the first time I understood what he truly meant by this. People are heaven's treasure, and Hazel and I will be connected for all of eternity. I can't wait to reunite with Hazel in heaven and hear all of the other details of the story of how our paths crossed one fateful evening at a sleepy old church in Durham, NC and how God used it to change both of our lives forever.

Chapter Two

Unlikely Grace

I WILL NEVER FORGET the first time I saw the girls. It was the fifth night of the tent revival and things weren't going as planned—or at least how I had planned. We had begun on a Friday and garnered a decent turnout through the weekend. We even had a reporter from the Post and Courier, our local newspaper, come out with a photographer to write a story for the following Sunday's paper. That night, I baptized a family of six, a single mother with her five children who wanted to get her life right with God and her family back on track.

There were 300 chairs under the tent so even with the 50 or 60 people who came out the first two nights, the place still looked rather vacant. One of my intercessors who prayed over every single seat before we started each night told me not to worry about empty chairs because angels would fill them. I received the consolation but held on to hope that attendance would slowly grow until the tent was full. I imagined the tent at max capacity with every seat filled and the crowds pressing in on all sides to hear the good news being preached.

But when attendance began to dip rather than increase on Sunday and Monday nights, I started to lose faith and rather than seeing angels, I just saw a sea of empty folding chairs. Attendance on Tuesday night was the worst yet, and when 7:00 p.m. rolled around, I had to give my watch a double take because the tent was practically empty. I held off starting the meeting as long as I could to allow for a few more folks to trickle into the tent, but the worship team was ready and we had to get things rolling despite the embarrassment I felt for them playing almost quite literally to an audience of one.

Jesus once told a parable of a shepherd who left his flock of 99 sheep to go look for one mischievous sheep who had wandered off. The shepherd looked high and low, under and behind every bush and rock, searching with all of his might until he found the lost sheep, at which point he celebrated the recovery of his property.

Jesus then tells the story of a woman with 10 silver coins who loses one of them in her house. She searches high and low for the coin and when she finally recovers it, she calls her friends and neighbors together to rejoice over locating her lost possession. At the end of these two parables, Jesus makes this statement in Luke 7:10, "Just so, I tell you, there is joy before the angels of God over one sinner who repents."

People are treasure, and God's heart is for every single one of his children. The human race is so incredible, it defies description. We marvel at how no two snowflakes are ever alike or how no two zebras have the exact same pattern of stripes, but how far surpassing in wonder and awe is human diversity, that you could travel the globe and spend your entire life meeting people and never find two just alike.

Although deep down I knew how God's heart beats passionately for the one and that attendance and numbers did not matter to him, I could not seem to stave off the feeling of shame and embarrassment that gripped me in my gut over the poor turnout. I was embarrassed for the musicians and the volunteers who had generously donated their time, but mostly, if I was truly honest, I felt embarrassed for myself.

Sixty-five years earlier nearly to the day, Billy Graham began his famous crusade in Los Angeles that launched him into international stardom. Over the course of the eight week campaign, Graham spoke to an estimated 350,000 people at a time when the population of the entire city was less than 2 million. He started that crusade at the age of 30, the very same age I was at the start of this, my first tent gathering. A few of my close friends had pointed out similarities between the two of us which had sparked high hopes of a big turnout that would be the catalyst for further ministry.

If you had asked me at the time about the tent revival, I would have told you with all sincerity that my motives were pure. I knew that the chances of becoming the next Billy Graham were about as good as the kid in the park's chances of becoming the next Kobe Bryant, but still I longed to see those seats filled and to see lives changed in the same way mine was more than a decade prior.

Ever since that fateful day in the ocean when I peered across the thin veneer of death into hell itself, I had lived with an almost plaguing desire to see people come to know Jesus so they would not have to experience the horror of an eternity separated from God. It was the first thing I thought of when I woke up in the morning and the last thing I thought of when I went to sleep at night. I knew that all of the material things we spend our whole lives chasing would one day turn to dust, and at the end of the day, all that mattered would be the final verdict pronounced over us on the day of final judgment—heaven or hell.

There is an old missionary slogan that says, "May the lamb who was slain receive the reward of his suffering." The price that Jesus Christ paid and the suffering that he endured on the cross is completely incomprehensible to us. The one who created the heavens and the earth, the one who engineered the universe and all the galaxies, the one who lived in perfect peace with God the Father since before time began, that one died a bloody humiliating death on a cross in front of his closest friends and his worst enemies, that one went to hell so we wouldn't have to. There is no length he would not go (and did not go) for just one of his beloved children—the ultimate reward of his suffering.

As the worship music played, I got down on my knees at the foot of the giant wooden cross and began to repent before the Lord. I confessed the wrong motives that I had allowed to creep into my heart and asked for forgiveness. I wanted to live for the one, to have eyes for the one single precious human being who God may put in my path today, to stay focused on his pure heart for souls and not my fallen desire for success. I asked that he would take away the sense of embarrassment that I felt burning up my whole body and to give me his heart for the one.

I realized that rather than counting up the number of people in the tent, I had been counting down from 300. Or from 350,000. I suppose this is the snare of the American preacher, to equate success in ministry with a headcount like corporations do with their bottom line or nations with their GDP. It's amazing how our sinful nature finds its way into everything we do throughout our lives, to include, and maybe even especially, our service to God.

As I poured out my heart before the Lord, I could feel his love washing over me. He reminded me that he is still on his throne and that he has a plan. He loves the people of my city and my nation infinitely more than I ever will, and he knows every hair on every head. I began to find rest in my spirit and peace in my soul, and I decided that I would continue to spend my life helping whoever he brought my way, whether it is one or a million.

The worship music had been playing for quite some time and I knew that the musicians needed a break, so I slowly arose from the floor secretly hoping to find the tent full of people. Unfortunately or perhaps fortunately, it was still just as full of angels as before, but this time I was feeling much better in my heart about the whole situation. I got on the microphone and addressed the 20 or 30 people who were scattered throughout the first few rows of the tent. I closed my eyes and began to pray, this time aloud over the PA system.

I don't know how long I prayed, maybe it was two minutes and maybe it was ten, but suddenly I began to hear noises all around me. I opened my eyes and what I saw was etched into my memory forever. The tent was filled with young Black girls dancing and twirling and waving colorful worship flags of red, pink, blue, gold and purple. They were all moving together around the cross, holding the flags and dancing in sync with several ladies from the prayer team. Around and around they danced, flags flying high and arms raised in worship.

The movements were so harmonized and the scene so surreal that I almost couldn't believe my eyes. As I sat watching this spontaneous display of grace and beauty unfold, a friend came over and whispered in my ear. "When you were praying and you started talking about the angels," he said as the dance continued in front of us, "all these little girls just started filtering across the field." I have no recollection of praying anything about angels, but I knew this was an answer. And the best thing about these angels was that I could actually see them!

Due to the synchronization, I thought for sure the dance must have been rehearsed and choreographed, that perhaps this was some sort of youth group or dance team from a local church. I began to rack my brain. How did I miss this? I had organized every aspect of the tent revival and never had anyone mentioned praise dancers or a group of children coming to perform. But as I soon found out, no one in the tent that night had ever met any of these girls.

The American Heritage Dictionary defines grace as "seemingly effortless beauty or charm of movement, form or proportion." This was God's grace manifested in a way I had never before witnessed. There is something about watching young children worship God that refreshes the soul. The purity and the simplicity of the entire scene made my heart leap in a fresh new way. The girls danced with abandon and when they had finished, they all took a seat where the not-so-visible angels had been sitting before.

When I stood up to preach, suddenly the tent felt a whole lot less empty than before. This handful of girls along with the adults they had been dancing with filled up almost an entire row of chairs. I preached the gospel with gusto, as if I were Billy Graham preaching to the masses, and ended with an invitation for salvation. One of our prayer ministers who had been sitting with the girls informed me that the girls, all of them, wanted to be baptized.

After I had finished speaking, the worship team began to play again in the background and I pulled the group of young girls aside to talk with them and to share the gospel with them in the most basic terms. How God created all of us as his children and how we fell from grace through sin. How God sent his son, Jesus, to the Earth to save us from the curse of sin and death. How when we believe in Jesus, he promises to save us from an eternity in hell so we can live forever with Father God in heaven. And how, when we believe in Jesus, we go down into the waters of baptism to symbolize death to the old life of sin and self, and we come up cleansed, a new creation in Christ made for good works, to live the rest of our days for God and for others.

I asked each one if this is what they really wanted and if they were ready to commit their whole lives to Him. One by one they agreed and we prayed together that they all be born again. I told them that I would be happy to baptize them but that we would need to talk to each of their parents first, both for permission and to invite them to share in this significant moment in their daughters' lives. I sent the girls home that night not sure if I would ever see them again. Little did I know, my life would never be the same again.

THE HOT DOG MINISTRY

"I NEED TO GET SAVED."

I hadn't even stepped down from the concrete slab where I had just finished preaching to a crowd of homeless men and women waiting in line for a free hot dog when a gaunt man darted out of the crowd with the question already rolling off his tongue. His eyes were serious as death, and I could have known he was a Marine even before he told me.

"I tried this before," he continued. "But it's never worked, not for me." He went on to share that he had been diagnosed with cirrhosis of the liver and that his doctor had given him one month to live. He spent nine years in the military killing people for a living, and he shared that he had killed even more people since he got out. He told me that he needed to know just one thing, "Is there forgiveness for me?"

I had never seen this man before and his question caught me off guard. Usually, people didn't come over and talk with me until after they had gotten their food because once they broke from the line, they couldn't get their place back. As I gathered my thoughts, I looked out over the hot dog ministry where homeless folks gathered each night at 5:00 p.m. for a free meal on the empty lot by the old gas station on the corner of Meeting and Lee Streets in downtown

Charleston. The lot was owned by a generous local businessman, who graciously allowed us to use his property for the nightly outreach.

The scene was a phenomenon. At 4:45 p.m., the lot was almost completely empty apart from maybe one or two homeless men and a handful of seagulls. Then, in the span of a couple of minutes, scores of SUVs would appear out of nowhere carrying folding tables, propane grills, boxes full of hot dogs and buns, water coolers and cups, condiments, chips, cookies, a box of day-old pastries and occasionally some overripe fruit. In the heat of summer or when rain threatened, a couple of small collapsible tents covered the bulk of the operation.

At the very same time, streams of homeless and poverty-stricken individuals would begin to appear from all directions and form a line at the front of the head table where the grills were set up. Women and children were ushered to the front of the line while the men fell in behind them. Hungry and opportunistic seagulls waited eagerly on the concrete slab and in the surrounding trees for any leftovers that were dropped or, to the chagrin of the ministry founder, fed directly to them.

Remarkably, this ritual happened at the same time and place every single night of the week, rain or shine, barring Christmas and Thanksgiving only because meals were already being served elsewhere on those days. The official name of the organization was Barnabas Ministries, but everyone knew it simply as "the hot dog ministry."

The genesis of the nightly meal started with a single College of Charleston student who was sharing his Christian faith with a friend. His friend challenged him that if he really believed what he said then he should do something about it. So he bought a couple of packs of hot dogs, went out into the street and the rest was history.

The meal grew from one night per week to two to three to being a nightly occasion. By the time I came along, each night was sponsored by a different church group who were responsible for bringing their own food and cooking supplies. Without communicating with one another, each small group of volunteers had their place in the rotation and formed a seamless stream of meals throughout weeks and months and years like a colony of ants working together in perfect harmony.

Some of our guests came every night. Others showed up once or twice per week and still others would stop in for a meal never to be seen again. One thing that always impressed me was how overwhelmingly thankful our guests were for the meal. I heard again and again from individuals who told me that they wouldn't have eaten all day if it weren't for the ministry. Granted the menu was limited, but that didn't stop them from coming. On average, we would see 50-75 people come through on a given night, and with those who came back for seconds and thirds, we regularly dished out 300 plus hot dogs a night.

While most of the volunteers at the hot dog ministry found a role behind the table serving food or drinks or topping dogs with condiments, my job was a unique one. Five or ten minutes before the hot dogs were served, I stood up on edge of the concrete slab where everyone sat to eat their meal and I preached the gospel as loudly as I possibly could. My perch put me about one and a half feet higher than those standing in line, which was enough to see everyone clearly, but with the noise from the street traffic only about 20 feet away, I really had to give it my all to reach the entire crowd.

Jesus said that man can't live by bread alone, but by every word that proceeds from God. Giving food to a hungry person is a wonderful thing and it reflects God's heart of kindness and mercy. But just as our bodies need food, our souls need truth. I wanted to make sure that those who came out each night received both.

Some nights the line was longer than others. The crowd was generally the smallest around the first of the month when food stamps renewed and disability checks were mailed out. But as the month went on, attendance at the hot dog ministry and other free meals in town steadily grew. On nights when the line was really long, I would often find myself hoarse after just five or ten minutes of preaching. I wanted everyone to hear the message of hope that God loves each of us no matter what and to know beyond the shadow of a doubt that he is, as the psalmist says, "a very present help in trouble" (Psalm 46:1).

Street preaching did not come naturally for me. I tried to go to seminary four different times because I thought that's just what you did when there was a call of God on your life, but each time the Lord closed the door. Since I didn't have a church to preach in, I decided to go where the people were. I started sharing my story with the homeless and those who had been marginalized and tossed aside by a fast-paced society focused on efficiency and productivity.

I moved back home to Charleston when my dad got sick with cancer in 2008 and picked up where I left off in Durham. I began to attend homeless outreaches all over the city and, although there was no centralized location like the hill where everyone gathered, I began to get to know the men and women who roamed the streets of downtown.

One day at a homeless picnic, I felt a nudge in my spirit to stand up and start preaching. At first I figured it must have been a bad burrito and I ignored it, but the prompting did not go away. I was so embarrassed that I wanted to die, but I knew that I had to be obedient to the Lord, so I stood up on a bench and closed my eyes as tightly as I could and I recited 1 Corinthians chapter 13, which I had memorized in its entirety.

"Love is patient and kind; love does not envy or boast; it is not arrogant or rude. It does not insist on its own way; it is not irritable or resentful; it does not rejoice at wrongdoing, but rejoices with the truth. Love bears all things, believes all things, hopes all things, endures all things." As it turns out, I did not die, but I was quite happy when the ordeal was over.

The next week at the homeless picnic, the leaders shared that preaching didn't fit with their vision for ministry, but I could not shake the prompting of the Lord. I felt like Jeremiah who said that if he did not speak about the Lord, it was like "a burning fire shut up in [his] bones" (Jeremiah 20:9). I knew that I had to let what was inside of me flow out somehow, so I walked down to Meeting Street about 100 yards from the picnic, I stood up on a small ledge next to the sidewalk and I started preaching to cars as they passed by.

I bellowed as loudly as I could, quoting scripture and praying over the city, and when I would notice people walking by or cars stopped at the red light with their windows rolled down, I would suddenly get really quiet. Then once they were out of sight, I would start back up again. I eventually got somewhat comfortable sharing my faith in this public way, so as the Lord is prone to do when we get comfortable, he moved me to a much more well-trafficked spot, the Marion Square fountain on the corner of King and Calhoun.

I literally thought I was going to die from shame the first time I stood up to preach to a sidewalk full of pedestrians going out for a drink or a bite to eat late on a Friday night. A cradle Episcopalian, I had literally never seen a street preacher before in my life nor had it ever crossed my mind to become one. But I knew this was my assignment from the Lord, and he was faithful to increase my boldness until it became second nature to stand up and in a very literal way, perform the great commission by proclaiming the gospel to the whole creation. So by the time I got to the hot dog ministry, I only got a little knot in my stomach when I stood up to preach instead of a giant one.

"I just want the peace," the man standing before me finally shared, and my mind kicked into gear. I set my gaze on his narrow and serious face and looked deep into his bloodshot eyes. My heart went out to him. I swallowed hard and assured him that the answer was yes, that there is forgiveness through the cross of Jesus Christ and that he is Prince of Peace.

I told him that there is no sin too great for the blood of Jesus. Through his death on the cross, Jesus Christ paid the penalty for all sin, for all men, for all time, and he offers eternal life to all who repent and believe in him. On and on I went, sharing the gospel up and down, left and right. Yet despite my words, he could not seem to get over his past, bringing up story after story after story. Someone he had killed, someone else he had beaten up. Each time, I told him that there is no sin too great for the Lord Jesus Christ. Were my words getting through at all? I wondered. I could feel the heavy weight of sin he had been carrying for a long, long time and knew he had to get a release.

I had no more words for the man, so I invited him to kneel with me. This was the only way I knew to get to God, through repentance, through kneeling at the cross, through laying my sins bare before the Lord, through the grace and mercy of my savior Jesus Christ, and it has always worked for me. On the surface, I was afraid that this man would walk away just like he came, bound up in unforgiveness, filled with sorrow, eaten up by regret. But deep down, I knew that it would work for him too. I knew that if he came honestly before the Lord, he would get the peace he was looking for.

We knelt together on the hard concrete slab with no cushion and no kneelers. The man's knees were so bony that I almost felt sorry for him, but before I even had time to think about lending him a hand, he hit the deck. Most people kneel slowly and cautiously on hard surfaces like this one, but this man did not hold back and laid himself before the Lord with his face to the ground.

I gently placed my hand on his back and began to pray that the Lord would release His Spirit of repentance and conviction over him. After I finished praying, I gave him the same instructions that I give to everyone I meet who wants to be born again. Rather than having him repeat a prayer in my words, I told him to pray in his.

"Tell the Lord what's on your heart in your own words. He's your Father and He wants to hear from you. There's no wrong answer, just be honest and do business with God." I prayed quietly to myself and waited as a couple of minutes went by. Then an incredible thing happened.

"I have the peace!" he exclaimed.

Before I even had a chance to get up, my new friend was on his feet. I quickly clamored to my feet and began to ask him what had happened. He told me that he felt peace in his heart, that the weight he had been carrying all these years was finally gone and that he felt clean. He had a new lightness about him and his face even looked radiant. All of the signs pointed to one thing, but since it's not my job to tell somebody else if the Lord has touched them or not, I wanted to be sure that he got what he came for. "Are you saved?" I asked him. He paused for a moment.

"I believe I'm saved," he said rather reflectively.

You couldn't wipe the smile off this man's face if you tried, and I rejoiced in his breakthrough. I went on to explain the importance of baptism and how nowhere in the book of Acts did the first disciples wait to baptize a new believer. He had been cleansed on the inside by the righteous blood of Jesus Christ, and his sins had been washed away for all eternity. The Lord had even allowed him to tangibly feel this cleansing in his soul. Now he would be washed in the waters of baptism as the outward seal of this inward exchange.

I asked him if he was ready and he agreed, so I looked around and headed straight for the only water I could find, a cup of drinking water that the volunteers had set out on a table for the guests. I poured the water over his head three times and baptized my new brother in the name of the Father and of the Son and of the Holy Spirit.

A few volunteers had gathered around us by this point, so we laid hands on and prayed together for him to receive the gift of the Holy Spirit. We prayed for his complete healing and I told him that if God would so graciously touch his soul that he would also heal his body. He began thanking and praising God with us and lifted his hands up to the King of Kings and Lord of Lords.

He had mentioned earlier that he needed to leave early, so we exchanged phone numbers and he left praising God. Then I realized something. He had never even gotten a hot dog!

Poverty or Oppression?

Over the next few years, my heart for the homeless led me to all of the haunts in the inner city where the homeless seek rest (or as much rest as you can get sleeping in a back alley or on a park bench) and even more so where they seek food. Free meals are always on the radar for the homeless, and they plan their days and weeks around where they can find the nutrition needed to survive.

Only a few blocks away from the hot dog stand, there is another free meal on the Eastside which has been running continuously every Monday to Friday for nearly 100 years. The official name of the ministry is Sisters of Charity of Our Lady of Mercy, but everyone just calls it "Sisters" because it is operated by two nuns who have been there as long as anyone can remember.

At 12 o'clock on the dot, a plain black door on the side of a large Catholic church that no longer holds services swings open, and the homeless and low income folks who have gathered outside begin to file into an underground room adorned with rows and rows of folding tables surround by folding chairs, six or eight to a table.

The assortment of folks who come through the line is impressively diverse, from chronically homeless seniors, to teenagers who have aged out of the foster system, to garbage men and other city workers stopping in for a free lunch. At Sisters, no one is turned away and although I have heard some complaints about the food, most seem to be genuinely thankful. They even send everyone away on Friday with a bag lunch to help them make it through the weekend.

In addition to the hot dog ministry and Sisters both being located on the Eastside, the neighborhood is also home to the only free homeless shelter in the Charleston area, making the Eastside a major artery for homeless foot traffic downtown. My passion to serve the homeless naturally drew me to the area, and I spent a lot of time in the Eastside community (and all over creation) helping those who were in complete crisis mode with nowhere to lay their heads and with no one to help them navigate the steep and slippery slope back into life indoors.

After being married in 2011, my wife and I found an apartment right around the corner from the hot dog stand and joined a small, Black church on the Eastside with the hopes of having a home base to minister to the homeless and the poor. We started a homeless brunch on the first Saturday of the month with a service beforehand including a time for worship and a message of hope. We distributed clothes and blankets and sleeping bags when it got cold and always tried to connect the homeless with shelter and the services they needed around the city.

The message of Isaiah 58 and Matthew 25 continued to resonate inside of me on a daily basis as we attempted to meet both the physical and spiritual needs of the poor. The Lord showed me a parallel in these passages between the natural and the supernatural, the both/and of the gospel, calling us to feed his children with natural food and the Word of God, to give them natural drink and the water of life, to cover their nakedness with natural clothes and with his robe of righteousness, and to welcome the homeless and the stranger into our natural homes and to bring them into God's house, the eternal kingdom of heaven.

Jackie Pullinger, who has spent over 50 years of her life ministering to the poor in Hong Kong, shared about food lines, that "the meal is as important as the prayer." When a brother or sister is hungry and hurting, we can't neglect their physical need. But once we take care of that physical need, God's mercy and compassion working through us gives us a natural platform to meet their spiritual needs as well.

Yet as I spent more and more time on the Eastside, I began to pay attention to the neighborhood itself and the permanent residents who called this small, two-and-a-half square mile portion of the Charleston peninsula home. Just three miles from the South of Broad neighborhood where my grandparents, my parents and my entire extended family hailed from, the two communities were worlds apart.

Unlike the immaculately cared for homes I grew up in and around, I saw paint peeling and roofs caving in, windows boarded up and vines climbing everywhere they found a place to climb, rusted out chain link fences enclosing dirt yards, old appliances and oven stoves sitting in driveways, cracked and broken plastic chairs masquerading as porch furniture. I saw a neighborhood that was all Black with not a White face to be seen anywhere except for the police officers who continually patrolled the streets.

I saw single moms trying to juggle full-time jobs on top of full-time households. I saw fathers struggling to make ends meet and rotating in and out of prison. I saw young children running the streets without any parents or adults around, kids taking care of kids, children toting around toddlers and sometimes infants, all roaming the same streets and sidewalks where the homeless traveled back and forth to their free meals. I saw little boys riding pink and purple bikes two sizes too small and little girls with no bikes to ride at all.

I saw young and middle aged men walking with canes or riding in wheelchairs. I saw teeth missing. I saw the ravaging effects of chronic obesity and diabetes from poor nutrition. I saw how few people had reliable transportation and how it seemed that most residents walked or biked to where they needed to go. I saw women carrying bags of groceries on foot, something I had never had to do in my entire life, or taking their laundry in sacks or on carts to the laundromat, a place I had literally never set foot in before.

At first glance, the absence of cars and washing machines did not seem like that big of a deal. But then I began to think about navigating my own life without them. How would I get to work or to church or to wherever else I wanted to go without a car? Not that I would have anything clean to wear anyway without a washing machine. I could figure out the bus route, but who has time to wait on the bus?

The lack of resources in the community went far beyond transportation and at times was staggering to witness. I remember being in a project apartment where two of the girls lived and hearing the incessant chirp of the smoke detector sounding off every minute or so. I knew it was only a low battery, so I went straight home and grabbed a nine-volt battery in order to make the painful noise stop and to make sure these girls had a working smoke detector in their home. When I went back and told the girls' mom what I was planning to do, she told me not to bother, that the thing had been beeping for over a year.

I insisted and quickly climbed the stairs before I faced any more resistance. There were no lights at the top of the stairs or anywhere else in the house for that matter, so I had to use a flashlight to even see what I was doing. After replacing the battery, I enjoyed a moment of silence and was celebrating this small victory when I heard the exact same loud chirp, only slightly muffled. I looked up at the smoke detector and could see that the battery was good. Then I realized the noise was coming from the smoke alarm next door.

As I pondered this world without light bulbs or batteries, I began to ask some hard questions. How has this neighborhood remained so poor while the rest of the city is literally booming all around it? How have the divisions of rich and poor and White and Black remained so distinctly delineated 150 years after the Civil War and 50 years after the Civil Rights Movement? Why are the generations so short here, and where on earth are all of the fathers?

I knew all too well what poverty looked like, but this was something different, something more. Poverty can happen to anyone. You lose your job or you fall on hard times, then one thing leads to another and you end up on the streets. Like the nurse I met who ran over a guy and killed him on her way home from a late shift. Even though the accident wasn't her fault, she was so torn up with guilt that she was unable to work and ended up just a couple years later homeless and sleeping in a tent.

Or the contractor who got t-boned by a car that ran a red light, shattering five of his vertebrae. The doctors literally could not do anything for him except to put a rod in his back just to keep his spine together. Since he wasn't able to work and didn't want to be a burden on his family, he checked himself into the local homeless shelter and spent his days lying in the bed of his pickup truck because it was the least painful way to pass the time.

I have heard it said that homelessness can happen to anyone, and after more than a decade of homeless ministry, I believe it. Just as Job understood after losing all of his family and wealth in an instant, "the Lord gives and the Lord takes away."

Poverty is no respecter of persons. Sometimes it results from misfortune and other times from poor planning. Yet what I saw as I looked deep into the face of the Eastside neighborhood was something deeper. This was systematic poverty, generational poverty. The depth and breadth of scarcity that existed across the board in this community wasn't a result of bad luck or poor planning—it was a product of historic oppression.

As I prayed over the community, the Lord took me back to Isaiah 58, to the very scripture that he had used to capture my heart and launch me into homeless ministry so many years ago. I had long understood Isaiah 58:7, the importance of feeding the hungry and clothing the naked and providing shelter for the homeless. But I had never been able to grasp verse 6: "Is not this the fast that I choose: to loose the bonds of wickedness, to undo the straps of the yoke, to let the oppressed go free, and to break every yoke?" (Isaiah 58:6)

This verse had always seemed so intangible to me. What on earth were "bonds of wickedness" and "straps of the yoke"? Who exactly were the "oppressed" and how was I going to "let them go free"? I knew that poverty was a problem in the inner cities of America, but oppression? Last I checked, Civil Rights was a done deal. This is the 21st Century, I thought, oppression is a thing of the past.

Yet as I began to dig beneath the surface, what I found truly shocked me to my core, and it turned my whole world upside-down.

Revisiting American History

Although I felt like I had a pretty good grasp of the American narrative from my high school and college history classes, I wanted to revisit our national storyline through the lens of Black history to help me fill in some of the gaps that I was seeing on the Eastside. I had read about slavery and Jim Crow in school, but I felt like there was a disconnect in my mind between then and now. If the struggle for Civil Rights was over and done with more than 50 years ago, why are we still seeing such stark racial disparities in our culture today?

As I began to read up on the history of the Black community in this nation, it didn't take long before my boat got rocked. I would get on my computer hours before my kids woke up (at 7:00 a.m. on the dot), and I would cry as I read story after story, account after account of unbelievable atrocities committed on the very soil where I have spent my entire life.

Morning after morning, I literally could not believe what was presented before me in black and white. The more I read, the more I began to see a new American narrative unfold. It was a history that I simply did not have eyes to see before, one which was not so neat, tidy and sterile as what the grade school textbooks had presented to me throughout my childhood and early adulthood.

The first thing I discovered is that oppression existed in the Americas long before any Africans ever set foot on these shores. While it is true that many settlers came to the New World solely for the purpose seeking religious freedom (as the oversimplified elementary school narrative goes), economic gain was undeniably the central driving force behind European colonization of the Americas, and the quest for profit dominated the overall culture in which both religious and non-religious settlers lived.

UNLIKELY GRACE

It's easy for us to picture the pilgrims in their funny little hats sailing on their funny little boats with triangular shaped sails on their quest for a place to worship God without persecution, and I believe that's the very point of a white-washed version of history. It creates a storyline that is simple enough for children to process, allowing them to come away with a visual image that their young minds can grasp without producing any conflicting feelings of cognitive dissonance. Yet it's much harder and morally messy to envision the true state of colonial North, South and Central America as it existed in reality.

For instance, I remember reading about Christopher Columbus and memorizing the little ditty about 1492 being the year that he sailed the ocean blue. I knew that he did not actually discover America, but I did not know that he and his men enslaved, raped and killed thousands of the Natives they encountered in the Caribbean where they landed. Columbus himself journaled about capturing girls as young as nine and ten years old and selling them as sex slaves, a shocking fact to uncover about a man whose birthday is celebrated to this day as a national holiday.

I vividly remember the Pilgrims and Indians play that our elementary school put on each year telling the story of the first Thanksgiving, but I do not recall learning about the tens of thousands of Native Americans who were enslaved and exported to the Caribbean as African slaves were being imported onto American soil.

Although I always associated the African slave trade with the genesis of slavery and oppression in the New World, it is evident from the lives of the earliest explorers and settlers that both slavery and oppression were a fundamental part of the European culture which was exported to the Americas. From the Portuguese sugar cane plantations in modern-day Brazil to the Spanish silver mines in Central and South America, the enslavement of both indigenous and

African people fueled European colonization of the New World. To know that slavery existed as a core institution in the Americas more than a century before the first African slaves landed in the colonial United States in 1619 is telling of the mindset which our earliest settlers carried.

While the concept of condoning slavery in any fashion is inconceivable to our 21st century minds, to those who arrived here in the 1500s and 1600s, slavery was simply a part of human life. From the Great Wall of China to the Hanging Gardens of Babylon to the Great Pyramids of Egypt, every empire in the history of the world up to that time had been built and maintained with slave labor.

The British Empire operating in North America proved to be no exception. For more than 250 years, chattel slavery persisted as the economic powerhouse which, combined with the rich natural resources discovered on American soil, fueled the extremely profitable English colonization of North America and eventually the rise of the United States as a global super power.

Despite the cultural familiarity surrounding it, American chattel slavery was a shockingly harsh and humiliating institution. I remember reading about the horrors of the middle passage and the desperate life of the American slave, but no history book I ever read in school described the half of what these poor souls endured, nor perhaps could any words ever record the true horrors in a book.

From the endless hours of backbreaking labor, to the meager provisions of food and clothing, to the physical and verbal abuse of the men, to the sexual abuse of the women, to the systematic breaking up of slave families, to the looming possibility of being sold and completely uprooted at any time for any whimsical reason, to the looming possibility of being tortured or killed at any time for any whimsical reason, to the knowledge that your children and grandchildren and great grandchildren would suffer the exact same fate into perpetuity, American chattel slavery is completely unimaginable and utterly unfathomable to anyone living in 21st century America.

In South Carolina, a revision to the slave code passed in 1739 prohibited slaves from working more than 15 hours per day in the summer and 14 hours per day in the winter. The fact that this had to be written into law is telling of the demanding nature of the institution and difficult to believe considering that working a human being beyond this point would almost certainly result in death.

It is reported that many Europeans who visited America were surprised by the number of mulatto slaves living in the American colonies. The rampant sexual abuse of female African slaves is one of the most glaring omissions from the sterilized textbook history of American slavery, and it produced a tangled web of genetics that implicates farm hands to presidents. Having intercourse with female slaves was not considered rape but rather a right of ownership. And the fate of the mulatto slaves is a tragic tale as slave-owners allowed their own flesh and blood to enter into and endure the harsh bonds of perpetual slavery, driven by a lust for both erotic pleasure and economic gain.

While slave conditions varied greatly from plantation to plantation and from small farm to small farm, chattel slavery even in the most ideal setting was a horrendous institution. Slaves were torn from their homeland and held against their will in shackles and chains crying out for the most basic of all human desires—freedom. A prevalent argument of the day was that slaves were better off under their master's care because at least their basic needs were met. But the intangible threat of being sold or having your spouse or children sold at any moment and never seeing your loved ones again negates any benefits slaves may have enjoyed within their bondage. Basic provision is no substitute for freedom.

Yet perhaps the most tragic and unashamedly evil aspect underlying the entire institution of slavery was the dehumanization of the slave. If a slave could be reduced to animal property in the mind of the culture, it made the inhumane treatment which he or she received tolerable to the slave master, the slave driver and the population as a whole. Even those who did not own slaves operated under this presumption in order to have peace of mind about the social order in which they lived. Without this mindset, American chattel slavery would have been a very difficult practice to implement and enforce.

This is the same psychological shift that occurred in Nazi Germany and in many other notable instances throughout the history of the world. Once a person is dehumanized and their basic humanity is stripped away in the eyes of their peers, the door is opened to a level of evil that is not possible for the average person to carry out otherwise.

Due to the dehumanization of the African slave, brutal and humiliating punishments such as whipping, branding, mutilation, sterilization, experimentation and murder were all common practices to keep chattel slaves in their proper place. Keeping slaves ignorant was another aspect of their degradation, and in most states, harsh penalties existed for teaching a slave to read or write.

On Ashley Avenue at the entrance of Charleston's Westside neighborhood, the road splits around "the old hanging tree," where a number of slaves were executed for insurrection. Some believe that this tree is where Denmark Vessey and 34 of his followers were hung after a failed slave revolt in 1822. It stands to this day as a reminder of the violent roots of American chattel slavery.

Tragically, the mindset of dehumanization toward African slaves bled into our most important and foundational documents—the Declaration of Independence and the United States Constitution. It is what allowed the founding fathers to hold in their hearts as self-evident truths "that all men are created equal" and "that they are endowed by their Creator with certain unalienable Rights, that among these are Life, Liberty and the Pursuit of Happiness" in a land where roughly half a million men and women—20 percent of the entire population—lived as slaves without any liberty or ability to pursue happiness at all. "All men" simply did not apply to slaves because slaves were property, the mental delineation that greased the wheels of the chattel slavery machine.

We know from God's word that all of His children are precious in his sight and that he does not look on our outward appearance, but rather on the heart. We know that there is neither Jew nor Greek and neither slave nor free in Christ. We know that every tribe and tongue will worship the Lord before his throne in his eternal kingdom and that every shade of skin color imaginable will be represented in that great congregation.

Yet because of the mindset that our earliest European settlers and founding fathers carried into the creation of our nation, they were not able to see God's likeness in Native American or African slaves. Instead, they saw them as animal property. This flaw in their thinking left a blemish on the formation of the United States of America which has been both a thorn in our side and a log in our eye, leading to the bloodiest and most divisive internal conflicts in our history—and persisting even to this day.

JIM CROW SOUTH

AS I CONTINUED TO STUDY our history as a nation, I routinely found myself shocked at what I discovered. It was like reading it all for the very first time, which led me to one of two conclusions.

Either I did not pay careful enough attention in high school history class (which is probably true for most of us if we are perfectly honest) or else there were some gaping holes in the history that was presented to me and to my generation.

Following the Civil War, a door of hope was cracked for the Black community in the South with the advent of the Thirteenth, Fourteenth and Fifteenth Amendments. It appeared that a new day had dawned for former slaves, and sweeping societal change seemed imminent. Yet after only a decade, the Reconstruction movement was essentially blocked by the Southern powers that be, and through violence, intimidation and extensive voter fraud, the all-White Democratic Party regained political control across the entire South, ushering in the cruel and twisted era known as Jim Crow.

Through an array of Jim Crow legislation, all of the rights that were guaranteed to the Black community on the Federal level were eventually negated by state and local laws mandating segregation in all realms of society. Although the Jim Crow South was definitely separate, it was light years from equal. The prevailing mindset in the Southern states during the age of chattel slavery spilled over into roughly 75 years of degradation and humiliation of freed slaves and their descendants that is hard to stomach from a humanitarian perspective. The basic humanity of Black people continued to go unrecognized in the mind of the majority of Southerners, allowing the strange social structure known as Jim Crow to rule and reign until the mid-1960s.

A Black neighbor once told me a story about growing up in Charleston during Jim Crow. He remembers as a 10-year-old boy that his father and his uncle used to alternate staying up all night on their porch watching over the house. They had White neighbors on both sides and one had threatened to burn their house down, so they resolved that someone had to keep watch at all times. With tears in his eyes, I could feel the pain and the sadness and even more so the confusion that this little boy must have felt as he was trying to make sense of a world in which the social and political structure essentially negated Jesus' most basic commandment to love our neighbor.

Just as in the era of chattel slavery, the strange code of Jim Crow which governed the South was enforced partially by law and partially by violence and intimidation. According to the Equal Justice Initiative, nearly 4,000 Black individuals were lynched during the height of Jim Crow, a form of public execution which often entailed torturing, burning, castrating or disfiguring the victim's body in broad daylight. These events were often publicized ahead of time, photographed and commemorated as postcards, which were later shared through the mail. Children and even infants were regularly brought with their families to these spectacles, regarded by many at the time as a form of sport.

The social caste system developed through slavery continued full force throughout the entire reign of Jim Crow. Signs reading "Whites Only" or "Colored" littered the Southern landscape dividing access to restrooms, water fountains, housing, schools, movie theatres, swimming pools and just about every public venue imaginable. Blacks were forced to step off the sidewalk, move to the back of the bus and essentially jump whenever any White person said jump. Noncompliance even in the smallest detail came at the risk of violent retaliation toward the individual and often their entire family. And since Blacks were barred from jury duty, Whites who committed hate crimes nearly always got off scot-free.

Aside from the humiliating social stipulations, the oppressive political restrictions, and the constant threat of violence toward anyone who stepped out of line, the economic ramifications of Jim Crow proved to be perhaps the most devastating aspect of this dark period in American history. Following the Civil War, the primarily agricultural Southern economy depended on cheap labor to function, and former slaves were still the primary engine.

Although many freed slaves fled plantation life and migrated north, these refugees had a difficult journey ahead of them with no resources whatsoever, leading to high rates of sickness and death. For the majority who stayed on the plantations, conditions did not change much. The sharecropping system which emerged was essentially a form of debt slavery where former slaves paid most, if not all, of their wages back to the land owner to cover the cost of equipment and basic needs.

Additionally, vagrancy laws were passed in the majority of Southern states which made unemployment a crime for Blacks and enabled authorities to arrest former slaves for minor infractions. This led to the leasing of hundreds of thousands of Black convicts to private companies for nominal wages where they were forced to work in conditions strikingly similar to those of the peculiar intuition of slavery, to include wearing fetters and working in "chain gangs."

Plantation owners during slavery had a vested economic interest in keeping their slave "property" as healthy as possible, but since there was no such incentive through the convict leasing system, working conditions were often worse and more inhumane than prior to the Civil War.

My mentor and former pastor, Brother Dallas, who has lived and served on the Eastside for more than 25 years, once told me: "If you emancipate someone but don't give them any land or resources to exercise their freedom, then they aren't truly free at all." This proved to be the case for nearly all former slaves who remained in the South following the Civil War.

The economic hurdles facing the Black community during Jim Crow were far-reaching, and the government was little help. When the New Deal legislation was drafted and implemented in the 1930s, Southern Democrats used their filibustering power to exclude farm workers and maids from all benefits, which comprised the vast majority of all Black laborers in the South.

Although the language was technically colorblind, the intention was clear and the ramifications were vast. As a result, the Black community was largely left out of the biggest government stimulus package ever conceived in this nation up to that point, effectively ensuring that Black labor would remain cheap and readily available at least for another several decades.

Following World War II, the advent of the G.I. Bill created sweeping prosperity across the nation for veterans returning home from Europe. Once again, Black veterans were excluded from benefits due to the way the bill was administered under Jim Crow and in many segregated areas in the North. As a result, the already stark wealth divide between White and Black grew exponentially during the Jim Crow era, and the majority of Black America remained economically stuck while the rest of the nation soared into unprecedented economic prosperity.

After decades of resistance, Jim Crow began to crack and eventually crumble with President Truman's executive order to desegregate the military in 1948, followed by the US Supreme Court case *Brown v. Board of Education* ending school segregation in 1954. The Civil Rights Act of 1964, the Voting Rights Act of 1965 and the Fair Housing Act of 1968 put the nail in the coffin of Jim Crow, officially marking the end of legalized segregation in the South. The gains were the fruit of a hard fought, nonviolent Civil Rights Movement led by Dr. Martin Luther King Jr, Rosa Parks, Charleston's own Septima Clark and countless others who sacrificed their bodies, and often their lives, for the sake of attaining freedom and equality.

Despite legal and political victories, the response of the Southern White community was only further resistance. Throughout the 50s and 60s, violent attacks against the Black community and those active in the Civil Rights Movement in particular ramped up dramatically as Black churches, which were hubs of community activism and organization, were bombed and burned to the ground. Civil rights workers faced the same terror that was used to intimidate quote carpetbaggers and scalawags (as well as any freed slave who got involved in the political process) during the Reconstruction era a century before.

But almost more devastating than the acts of violence perpetrated by White terror groups, the response of the White community at large revealed that no real change of heart had occurred in regards to segregation. The massive immigration of Whites from racially mixed urban areas into nearly all White suburbs known as "White flight" had a demoralizing social and economic impact on the impoverished Black community, gutting the inner city of commerce, development and tax revenue for essential city services.

While federally insured and subsidized mortgages opened the door for White families to easily relocate to newly formed suburban communities, exclusionary covenants and discriminatory practices such as redlining ensured that Black families remained left behind in a world increasing categorized by urban decay. Of the $120 billion worth of home loans backed by the federal government between 1934 and 1962, more than 98% went to White homebuyers.

And while the Interstate Highway System provided an avenue for White commuters to quickly access the positive benefits of city life without having to live there full-time, the very same roadways blazed straight through poor Black communities in cities all across the nation, destroying historical landmarks and dividing families, friends and neighbors.

In Charleston, the Crosstown Expressway which opened in 1968 tore right through the predominantly Black Eastside and Westside neighborhoods, leaving 150 houses demolished in its wake. Increased traffic noise and pollution decreased the quality of life around the six-lane highway, and a virtual wall was created further segregating the northern and southern halves of the peninsula.

The empty lot where I held the tent revival marked the old footprint of the Crosstown before the new Cooper River Bridge redirected the traffic pattern in 2005. Less than two blocks from where each of the girls called home, the high-speed freeway stood as a constant reminder of racial bias from the Halls of Congress, where the Federal-Aid Highway Act was passed, to the local community, where walking to grandma's house—or worse, daddy's apartment—was no longer a reality because of an uncrossable asphalt barrier.

One of the major catalysts for White flight was the desegregation of public schools set in motion by *Brown v. Board of Education* in 1954. Following the ruling, Southern leaders fought tooth and nail against the desegregation process and successfully resisted for an entire decade. But with the passing of the Civil Rights Act of 1964, which granted governmental authority to defund entire school districts that did not comply with integration, segregated private schools became the new battle plan and began to spring up like wildfire all over the nation literally overnight.

In the matter of a few short years, hundreds of thousands of White students from elementary to high school were pulled out of the public school system and enrolled in all-White private schools. Many of these schools, dubbed "segregation academies," had racially discriminatory enrollment policies prohibiting Blacks from attending. Others simply used tuition as a financial barrier to entry, which is still the primary agent of school segregation to this day. It wasn't until 20 years after *Brown v. Board of Education* that segregated private schools were ruled unconstitutional by the Supreme Court in 1976.

Growing up, it never occurred to me that a private Episcopal school being founded in 1964 carried any significance whatsoever. It certainly wasn't mentioned in any the school's history that I ever read. Yet it would be a hard case to make that the timing was a coincidence. Nor was it a coincidence that there was not a single Black person in my graduating class.

At a time when most paved roads ended where Black neighborhoods began and where basic services such as water, sewer, electricity and garbage pick-up served only the White parts of town, White flight was a devastating response to the Civil Rights Movement. Rather than running to the aid of the most impoverished communities in our nation, the White population as a whole turned a blind eye and ran in the opposite direction in order to carry on life, business and school as usual.

It is almost impossible for us today to understand the radical mindset shift that the American people and particularly those living in Jim Crow South had to undergo following the Civil Rights Movement. For centuries, White and Black people alike were told from the halls of political power to the church pulpit to the market-place that human beings of African descent were inherently less than those of European lineage and that we need to abide by this class distinction for the sake of our overall well-being. This message was drilled into the minds of everyone in the culture without exception from the time they were born to the time they died.

Then one day, the script was completely flipped. All of a sudden, the resounding message throughout the land was that Black people are inherently equal and that we all need to live together as one big happy family. Not only were they told that integration is now the right thing to do, they were forced to begin the process overnight.

The closest example of a comparably stark mindset transformation I can think of is that of Nazi Germany following World War II. During the years leading up to World War II and throughout the war (until the truth of Hitler's extermination camps was exposed), normal everyday German citizens watched as their Jewish neighbors were forcefully evacuated from their homes and marched down the street never to be seen again.

No one knew for sure where they were being taken, but they heard and believed the propaganda that it was an absolute necessity for the welfare of the entire nation to rid the land of the Jewish people. Although a small minority resisted the movement, the majority remained silent. Many looted and stole furniture and other valuables out of the empty Jewish homes.

Rumors spread about gas chambers and firing squads and mass graves, yet no one knew the truth for sure. Then one day, Allied soldiers showed up and uncovered the concentration camps, actually extermination camps, where millions of Jews were executed right under their noses. Can you imagine what was running through their minds as their few surviving neighbors returned home and tried to pick up life where they left off?

Immediately following the war, the process of denazification began as both the leaders and symbols of the Nazi movement were removed from their positions of prominence and erased from the public eye. But how can you wipe away a message and a worldview that had been drilled again and again and again into the minds of millions of people? You can take away the signs and the symbols overnight, but how do you change someone's heart?

The same process began in the post-Jim Crow South following the Civil Rights Movement. The "Whites Only" and "Colored" placards disappeared from restaurants and store fronts, hotel lobbies and bus stations, swimming pools and movie theatres, all in the blink of an eye. The lunch counters which had been the site of heated protests just weeks before were suddenly open to the general public—Black, White and every shade in between.

But the message of Black inferiority which had been hammered home for centuries wasn't quite as easy to erase from the public psyche. Throughout slavery and institutional segregation, an unceasing stream of propaganda was pumped into the hearts and the minds of White Americans from every possible avenue, cementing in the core of their being the absolute certainty that White and Black do not mix.

Thus, the response of the White community to the desegregation of America is not surprising. Since the government decided to no longer partner with their core conviction of segregation, they began to self-segregate. Historically, we can see with 20/20 vision that the Civil Rights Movement was morally right and completely inevitable, but to those who were actors on the stage at the time, desegregation was a war on their entire way of life.

CHAPTER THREE

TAKING THE PLUNGE

WHEN I ARRIVED AT the tent the first night after meeting the girls, they were already there waiting for me. The revival kicked off every evening at 7:00 p.m., but a group of us would gather an hour beforehand to pray. Although I had every intention of getting there half an hour early to be fully set up before prayer started, I typically arrived right at 6:00 p.m. and would pray as I unloaded the sound equipment and set up the stage. Trying to get out of the house with two-month-old twins and a one-year-old is no small task.

I pulled up to the edge of the empty lot where the tent stood, and just as suddenly as the girls had come into the tent the night before, they had completely encircled my car. I had to fight my way out of the door like a celebrity warding off the paparazzi at a red carpet event. I gave out hugs to all of the girls and then, as any task-oriented tent revivalist would do, I started unloading my car. That's when the questions began.

What's that thing? Do you have any microphones in there? Why is this so heavy? Can I carry something for you? I know they say that many hands makes light work, but when you are unloading a borrowed PA system that you would like to not drop so that you can return it in working order, the saying doesn't exactly apply. I gave the girls a couple of Tupperware bins to carry full of cords and cables and microphones, which at first they fought over and eventually carried over to the stage. Then they were right back at my side with more questions.

I did not realize how therapeutic and cathartic my normal and very quiet set up routine was until it had been bombarded. As an introvert, I always wondered why God had called me to street ministry and now a tent revival, but I learned a long time ago not to debate with the Lord. When I first started preaching the gospel, I thought for sure the butterflies in my stomach would go away at some point, but they never did. So I always enjoyed the calm before the storm of praying, and in this case setting up sound equipment, before it was my time to get on the microphone.

But any and all inconvenience aside, I was thrilled that the girls came back, and my heart was overjoyed to have them buzzing all around me like a busy bee hive. I had no experience with this age group except for spending time with younger cousins, but that generally came with the luxury of having their parents around. All of a sudden, I was thrust into the role of tent revivalist, stage manager and babysitter all at once.

In the world of street ministry, you typically see someone one day and they're gone the next. I remember baptizing a guy one time and asking for his phone number to discover that he didn't have one and then asking for his address to find out that he lived in a tent in the woods. But these little girls came back with bells on, and they were dressed and ready to be baptized.

Two of the girls who were sisters brought their aunt who gave permission on behalf of their mother who was working. Another pair of sisters got their mother on the phone who gave her blessing for the two of them, and one more of the girls was able to reach her mother who also agreed to allow her daughter to be baptized.

The other three girls could not get a parent on the phone for us to talk with, and although they begged me to baptize them anyway, I told them they would have to wait. The girls buzzed with excitement all throughout the opening time of worship, and when I finally took the stage, I knew that I needed to be short and sweet. I took a few moments to share about the ancient Christian sacrament of baptism and how it represents the washing away of all our sins and our rebirth into an entirely new life in God.

Jesus said that unless we are born again of water and the Spirit, we will never enter the kingdom of heaven. Baptism is the outward representation of what God does inwardly in our hearts when we repent of our sin and turn back to him. Baptism is so important to the Lord that Jesus himself submitted to it despite John the Baptist's initial opposition.

I can't say that I fully understand why Jesus told us to baptize new believers, but I do know that it is part of his very last instructions to his followers and who am I to challenge God's game plan? If it's important to him, then it's important to me. In fact, baptism became my primary measure of success each night. If I came home with wet clothes, my wife always knew that I would be happy.

Our baptismal pool was a miracle in and of itself. First of all, the guy who offered it to me had no idea that I needed one. And secondly, there was no water access on the property. We set it up by faith anyway and asked the Lord to provide the water. Later that day, an assistant fire chief pulled up right next to the tent. I thought he was going to arrest me for some safety infraction or not having enough lighted exit signs on the tent (like if the tent catches fire, please exit here or here). But instead, he simply asked if we needed anything. A couple of hours later, a fire truck pulled up and filled the small Jacuzzi-sized baptistry with water in just a matter of minutes.

After I finished sharing about baptism, we gathered everyone together, and one by one, these little girls affirmed their faith in Jesus. Although I had done street baptisms before, this was the first time I had ever had the luxury of using an actual pool. A cradle Episcopalian, I didn't even know that portable baptistries even existed. My general policy for baptism was to employ whatever water I could find. I have baptized people in four of our downtown fountains, and if there wasn't a fountain close by, I would use a pitcher or a cup or even a water bottle. My only goal was to get as much water on them as I could.

Since I had never baptized anyone full-emersion before the tent revival, my first few attempts were clumsy and comical. It was so bad that the crowd began spontaneously offering advice on dunking technique. But by the time I got to the girls, I had gotten some practice. I did not take into consideration how cold the water was, and it took some time sitting on the edge of the baptismal pool before the girls were ready to take the plunge. Yet each one persevered, and once it was all over, we gathered the whole group together to pray for these young women to receive the Holy Spirit, which is promised to all who believe and are baptized.

We baptized two more girls the following night and the last one two nights later. The beauty of watching these eight girls begin their spiritual journey and be baptized into a covenant life with their Heavenly Father was a blessing only paralleled by my own children's baptism. Just two of these eight girls had any type of consistent relationship with their biological father. But now all of them had been introduced to their true Heavenly Father who loved them before the world began. It is that love which set me free so many years before, and it was the greatest privilege in the world to share it with these amazing girls.

After the baptism, one of the grandmothers informed me that to her knowledge, these girls had never shown any interest in God or Jesus before the tent revival. She was amazed to hear that they all wanted to be baptized. For her, it was a pleasant surprise and something she had long been praying for. There's nothing more powerful in this world than a praying mother or a praying grandmother. Her prayers had been answered, and our journey was just beginning.

WAR ON POVERTY

FOLLOWING THE CIVIL RIGHTS ACTS of the mid-1960s, living and working conditions began to improve dramatically for the Black community in the South. New job opportunities opened up that had never before been available to people of color, and the previously stark wage discrepancy between White and Black workers began to close.

In the 30 year period between the outbreak of World War II and the passage of the long-awaited Civil Rights legislation, an estimated five million Black people left the South in what became known as the Great Migration on buses and trains in search of high paying jobs in the North, the Midwest and the West. But following the end of Jim Crow, the employment landscape improved for the Black labor force below the Mason Dixon Line, and they no longer had to travel hundreds of miles to find a decent wage.

In 1964, as a direct response to the Civil Rights Movement, Lyndon Johnson launched an all-out "War on Poverty" which was designed to eliminate racial injustice and reduce the poverty rate in America. In the center of this legislation, the Office of Economic Opportunity (OEO) was created to provide access for the poor to both quality education and employment.

Over the next few years, billions of Federal dollars began to flow directly into the most impoverished communities in the nation, to include historically Black neighborhoods all across the South reaching individuals who had never been eligible for Federal stimulus of any kind before. Before Johnson's Great Society, as it was called, nearly all Federal welfare assistance went to White individuals and families.

For example, the Aid to Dependent Children program created by the New Deal in 1935 was designed for White single mothers and excluded anyone who had previously been in the workforce, which ruled out virtually all Black single mothers. But with the advent of the Great Society, for the first time in our nation's history Black people began to receive Federal aid designed to help lift them out of their historic poverty.

In addition to the poor Black community, the OEO also targeted rampant and systemic poverty within the Native American community with the goal of combating illiteracy among children and increasing economic self-sufficiency among adults. Just like during Reconstruction following the Civil War, it appeared that a new ray of hope had broken through for African and Native American communities across the nation and particularly the South following the long and arduous battle for Civil Rights.

Yet from the start, Johnson's Great Society faced fierce backlash from the White community as well as a major hurdle in the form of the Vietnam War. Just a few years after its inception, the escalation of our conflict in Vietnam halted much of the domestic spending set in motion by Great Society legislation. A guns and butter debate raged on in the nation, and ultimately butter lost.

One source of conflict with the Great Society was the government's direct implementation of funds which bypassed state and local agencies. Under Jim Crow, nearly all Federal assistance programs were implemented locally to ensure the exclusion of Black individuals from all benefits. In order to prevent exclusion based on race, Johnson mandated that all Great Society funds would be administered to the recipients directly from the Federal government.

This created a great amount of friction and resentment within state and local agencies, creating a power struggle on top of already heated racial tension. An interesting parallel can be seen between the implementation and reception of the Great Society after Civil Rights and that of Reconstruction following the Civil War. Federal intrusion on the Southern way of life was met with resentment and resistance across the board from the White community.

Only five years after the full inclusion of the Black community into the Federal welfare system, conservative backlash led to the election of Richard Nixon as president, who ran on the platform of "abolishing the present welfare system and adopting a new one." Once in office, Nixon was true to his word, attempting to completely dismantle and defund the OEO. Rather than a War on Poverty, he declared a War on Drugs in 1971, citing that drug abuse was "public enemy number one."

For 30 years, New Deal and Fair Deal welfare programs helped alleviate poverty (and build wealth) among White families and individuals, but as soon as welfare assistance was opened to people of color, we voted as a nation for a complete overhaul of the system.

WAR ON DRUGS

ALTHOUGH THE LEGISLATION was technically colorblind, the War on Drugs from the very beginning was a targeted strike against the Black community. One of Nixon's top advisors, John Ehrlichman, later admitted that the primary impetus for the War of Drugs was to create a way to legally target and villainize hippies, who opposed the war in Vietnam, and Blacks, who opposed him politically.

"We knew we couldn't make it illegal to be either against the war or Black," Ehrlichman said in a 1994 interview, "but by getting the public to associate the hippies with marijuana and Blacks with heroin, and then criminalizing both heavily, we could disrupt those communities. We could arrest their leaders, raid their homes, break up their meetings, and vilify them night after night on the evening news. Did we know we were lying about the drugs? Of course we did."

Over the following decade and continuing on into the Reagan administration, legislation mandating harsh penalties for drug dealing and simple possession drastically changed the criminal justice landscape in America. The "tough on crime" language sounded good on the surface, but the racial profiling that came with it revealed the true heart of the legislation.

Suddenly, the policy focus coming out of the White House shifted away from alleviating historic poverty in Black communities to increasing the level of policing in those same communities. Rather than painting a picture of impoverished communities victimized by hundreds of years of oppression, poor Black communities were stigmatized as hotbeds of drug use and trafficking.

While statistically Whites and Blacks use drugs at comparable rates, Black people began to be (and still are to this day) arrested and incarcerated for drug offenses at astronomically higher rates than their White counterparts. The impoverished and abandoned Black inner city neighborhoods became flooded with police officers armed with paramilitary style equipment and firearms, and a literal war commenced.

While drug abuse continued to rage on in the White middle and upper middle class communities, the War on Drugs clearly displayed its racial and socioeconomic bias. Over the course of the 80s, 90s and 2000s, prisons across the nation were filled with Black and Brown men as a result of the intrusive policing tactics employed in low income communities of color. To this day, Black people are imprisoned at more than five times the rate of Whites.

At the same time White suburbs were flourishing with a level of prosperity never before seen in the history of the world, Black inner cities were turned into war zones. Black people were targeted and stopped on sidewalks, in their cars, at bus stations and everywhere in between. Their homes were raided, their children were targeted and their communities were occupied by SWAT teams armed to the teeth with assault rifles and riot gear. Once again, the dignity and safety of the Black community was compromised.

Can you imagine a report on the news about a White frat party getting raided by a SWAT team and a bunch of White university students being charged with felony drug charges? The Black ghettos were targeted for the same reason that the Interstate Highway System blazed right through the center of Black communities all over the country—it was the path of least resistance.

It is unimaginable to picture a drug raid of a White frat party, not because there aren't any illegal drugs to be discovered there, but because of how many lawsuits would be filed as a result. The War on Drugs naturally targeted the most vulnerable in our society because they are the ones with the least amount of legal and political recourse.

We know from the failed experiment of Prohibition in the 1920s and early 1930s that declaring war on a highly addictive substance is completely unsustainable and overall very harmful to society at large. Just as in the Prohibition era, the War on Drugs has led to a thriving black market as well as a rise in gang activity and violence surrounding the illegal drug trade. But because the middle and upper class White communities were the ones affected by Prohibition, it only lasted 13 years. Yet the War on Drugs has been devastating poor communities of color for nearly half a century—and counting.

Eroding the Fourth Amendment

What most people don't recognize about the War on Drugs is how it has dramatically shifted the nature of policing in our nation. Most crimes that are committed have a victim and they have a perpetrator. If you are the victim of a theft or a violent assault, you are going to be highly motivated to call the police and report the incident. In these and most criminal cases, the police are acting as responders to reported crime.

In the case of a drug deal on the other hand, neither party involved are likely to call the police because both the seller and the buyer are guilty of a crime. Even if theft or violent assault were to occur during a drug deal, those involved are still not likely to call the police because both sides would be implicated. Therefore, in order to wage a war on drug interactions, a completely different and intrusive style of policing is necessary.

Since the founding of this nation, American citizens have enjoyed the safeguard of the Fourth Amendment, which protects any citizen regardless of their status from "unreasonable search and seizure" with a very important built-in concept known as "probable cause." Essentially, in order for police to search my house, my car or my person, they have to provide good reason for why they are doing so. This concept dates back to the English common law dictum that "an Englishman's home is his castle."

Yet in order to find drugs on a person or in a car or in a home, police officers cannot sit back and wait. Suddenly, due to a Federal mandate making drugs our number one priority in policing, local police departments had to find proactive ways to locate drugs in their communities. Stop and frisks, traffic stops and home invasions in search of illegal drugs became the norm in American policing, and slowly but surely our Fourth Amendment rights were eroded completely away (although most middle and upper class White people weren't even aware that it was happening).

The entire prison population in the US in 1970 was just under 340,000 inmates. Today, there are more than 2.3 million people incarcerated in the United States, giving us the highest incarceration rate of any country in the world. It's like having the entire nation of Botswana imprisoned on our soil. Additionally, there are close to 1 million more on parole and another 3.7 million on probation, not to mention the countless millions of released felons who will never be able to fully integrate into mainstream society because of the mark on their very permanent criminal record.

I saw the ugly barred teeth of the War on Drugs and its aftermath through a Black friend in his early 20s named Anthony. He was a strong, attractive young man who attended our church and came regularly to my Tuesday morning Bible study. Every time I talked with him, he gave me a glimpse into the completely life-altering consequences of the drug war that no statistic could ever capture.

Anthony started selling crack cocaine at 10 years old, and by the time he was 12, he was paying most of the bills in his house with drug money. He had gotten into some trouble in his early teens but had managed to keep his freedom until he got caught at 18 with a small amount of drugs and a friend's handgun, which earned him a five-year Federal prison sentence.

Upon his release, he began to stay with relatives and look for a job, but with a felony conviction on his record, no one was hiring. He would walk up and down the street putting in applications to wash dishes at restaurants but rarely ever got a call back. When he overstayed his welcome at one place, which didn't take long with no money for rent or to even keep his cell phone on, he would move on to the next place. A young man in the prime of his life trying to do the right thing and work for a living, Anthony was met with nothing but closed doors and disapproving looks.

The War on Drugs has effectively targeted and criminalized entire generations of young Black men, labeling them as felons and locking them out of the economic mainstream for good. Before they even set foot out of their homes, they are already stereotyped and castigated as "less than," a banner they have lived under in this nation for nearly 400 years.

While many White people and individuals from other ethnic groups have been swept into the criminal justice system as a result of the War on Drugs, they are mostly from poor communities without the means to defend themselves in the court system, revealing that the War on Drugs is both a race war and a class war. Since Black and Hispanic people are much more likely to live in poverty than their White counterparts, the Drug War continues to impact their communities at a much higher rate.

I grew up in the 1980s and 1990s when the War on Drugs was being ramped up to its height, and I never once remember seeing a single police car in the all-White country club neighborhood where I grew up. Yet I can't drive on the Eastside of Charleston today without seeing one or sometimes two police cars on patrol. I understand now why that young boy thought my friend and I were from the Department of Corrections—it turns out they frequent his neighborhood quite often.

When I was at the peak of my drug addiction at age 20, I used to carry a bag of marijuana in my pocket everywhere I went. I never once thought that I might get stopped by a police officer and searched.

Even if I got pulled over for speeding, I knew that I would simply get ticketed and go my way. It never once occurred to me that I might be targeted by the police, even though I was technically a drug criminal.

At the same moment and completely unbeknownst to me, young Black men my same age were regularly being targeted and stopped by the police whether they used drugs or not. Right underneath the noses of middle class White America, the Drug War has ravished the poor Black community more than we can begin to fathom, and it is still raging on to this day. However, since it has not directly affected the mainstream American way of life, we have missed the heart cry of the Black community suffering at its merciless hand.

The shift from a war on historic poverty in the Black community to a discriminatory drug war just a few years after the close of the Civil Rights era effectively shut the door on the dawning of a new day in America. As the late rapper Tupac Shakur put it in his 1998 song, Changes: "Instead of war on poverty, they got a War on Drugs so the police can bother me."

The dream of Martin Luther King, Jr that his children would live in a nation where they were judged not "by the color of their skin but by the content of their character" quickly turned into a nightmare of a newly legalized form of racial profiling eerily similar to that of Jim Crow, rightfully earning the War on Drugs a painfully reminiscent moniker: "The New Jim Crow."

GLOBALIZATION AND WELFARE

AT THE SAME TIME the War on Drugs was ramping up, another national trend began to negatively impact impoverished inner city communities across the nation. Starting in the mid to late 1970s, prominent US companies began to outsource their manufacturing jobs abroad in order to save on labor costs, first to Mexico and Central America and then to Indonesia and China. This rising trend of globalization combined with the phenomenon of White flight, which shifted local commerce out of historic downtowns into suburban areas, created an employment vacuum in inner cities all across America.

Because education during the Jim Crow era was separate and far from equal, both in the South and in the North, the Black workforce was undereducated and depended largely on unskilled and semi-skilled labor jobs. When the manufacturing jobs began to dry up and much of the local business left the city centers, many Black individuals found themselves left out and left behind in an increasingly globalized economy.

For centuries, Black labor was the driving force of the United States economy. Violent oppression both during slavery and segregation ensured the availability of free, and later cheap, Black labor. Suddenly, cheap Black labor was replaced by even cheaper foreign labor in unseen pockets all over the world. Unskilled and undereducated Black workers underwent a shift from being oppressed to being marginalized—no longer needed and no longer sought after. As a result, the Black unemployment rate steadily grew throughout the 1970s and 80s, hitting a high of 19.5% in 1983 compared to 8.4% for Whites that same year.

Due to the high levels of unemployment and poverty in the increasingly marginalized inner city neighborhoods, two devastating trends were exacerbated. Black males with no available labor jobs turned more and more to a thriving black market for illegal drugs in order to survive, with huge percentages being swept into the criminal justice system, and Black females became increasingly dependent on a rising Welfare State, which promised to meet all of their needs as long as they remained unwed.

Taking The Plunge

I have a friend who was a social worker in Birmingham, Alabama in the early 1970s. She was given permission to search the closets of the welfare recipients she was assigned to, and if she found any men's clothing in them, she had the authority to cut off assistance. Since the economic landscape was so bleak in the inner cities and the money was so badly needed, she saw many instances of couples (even married ones) splitting up and the man moving out in order to avoid jeopardizing their welfare assistance.

Although the consequences were unintended, the welfare system drove a wedge right through the heart of poor Black families, and marriage rates began to fall steadily. In 1965, 24 percent of Black children were born out of wedlock. Today, that number has leapt to nearly 75 percent.

Ironically, both the War on Drugs and what remained of the War on Poverty had a destabilizing impact on the Black family, which functioned historically as the backbone of the Black community throughout both slavery and Jim Crow. During the long epoch of violent and bitter oppression, the Black family served as a refuge and a buffer against the hateful attitudes and actions that constantly bombarded people of color on a daily basis in American society.

The family was the one place where a person's inherent value and worth were recognized and reinforced despite the constant barraging lie of the culture that anyone with too much melanin in their skin was a second class citizen. And due to the outwardly violent nature of both slavery and Jim Crow, the Black family was actually strengthened and reinforced by the cruelty of the world outside, acting as a safe haven for all who were negatively impacted by an overtly racist culture.

Suddenly, the Black family, which had remained strong for centuries, began to unravel at the seams. With young Black men either leaving the community to find work, disappearing into the criminal justice system or losing their lives to the violence surrounding the illegal drug trade raging on in their backyards, young Black women had no other option but to remain unmarried and take the welfare subsidies offered to them. And with increased monthly assistance available for each additional child born into the home, the shortsighted incentive programs had completely predictable consequences.

Unlike the successful government assistance programs of the past like the New Deal and GI Bill which focused on asset creation through homeownership, entrepreneurship and secondary education (but excluded most Black people), the modern welfare packages we have seen over the past 50 years have actually worked against asset creation by penalizing hard work and marriage, the two most tried and true avenues for climbing out of poverty.

As a result, these programs have created a dependency on the state like never before seen in the history of our nation. Of course, poor White communities have been negatively impacted by the rise of the Welfare State, but since the rate of Black poverty is so much higher—more than twice that of White poverty in the United States today—the effects are more intensified in the Black community.

Forty Acres and a Mule

While it is easy to villainize communities of color for the resultant social ills which have arisen over the past half century out of a demoralizing Drug War and a rising Welfare State, the root of the problem is not social at all—it is economic.

The real underlying barrier to a successful transition for the Black community out of slavery following the Civil War and out of Jim Crow following the Civil Rights Movement was the complete denial of ownership in the mainstream economy.

Taking The Plunge

The institution of slavery in America barred the entire people group from land and property ownership for two and a half centuries. During the Reconstruction era, many slaves believed that they would be given the land that they and their forefathers had worked for so many years, only to have their hopes shattered.

The phrase "Forty acres and a mule" came from a promise made by the United States to redistribute land to freed slaves following the Civil War. Yet the Southern powers that be ensured that this promise never reached fulfillment, and instead, the vast majority of former slaves were employed on a wage system without any ownership of the land.

Throughout the entire oppressive era of Jim Crow, ownership of land, businesses and wealth of any kind continued to prove elusive for Black Americans. Although they were free in a legal sense, they were not free in an opportunistic one, that is, they did not have the recourse to pursue business opportunity because they had no property and therefore no leverage or ability to initiate capitalistic enterprise. And even when they did break into ownership opportunities, they regularly faced violence and intimidation which threatened to bring them right back down to zero.

Sharecropping was the only viable road to economic independence following the Civil War in the South, and it proved to be a particularly treacherous one, primarily because the White landowners still had absolute power to set the terms. And since most former slaves could not read or do basic math, the landowner had the final say on what was earned and what was owned when the accounts were settled.

As a result of the absence of Black ownership in the South, the unprecedented economic gains and prosperity of the 20th century remained for the large part in the same hands who had always owned and controlled the Southern economy—White land and business owners. Yet the irony should not be missed that every square inch of the land which the White community refused to share had been brutally taken from the Native Americans just centuries before.

With the lowering of barriers to international free trade following World War II and the establishment of an international commerce framework, multinational corporations began to spring up all across America and Europe. Due to the wealth creation in the White community through the New Deal, the Fair Deal and the post-war GI Bill, White households had more expendable capital than ever before, allowing for investment in these businesses which were prospering from the new rise of globalization. As a result, it was not only White executives and corporate employees who benefited from the rise of multinational corporations—the entire White middle and upper middle class had access to a slice of the pie through the stock market.

Yet for the majority of the Black community who were denied ownership for more than three centuries, there was no possible way for them to break into the economic gains that their White neighbors were able to reap through globalization. In fact, while the investments of the White community began to soar like never before, the labor jobs that the Black community depended on in the inner cities and elsewhere began to disappear overnight.

There is a story in the book of Genesis about Jacob laboring for his uncle, Laban, for 20 years before departing with his family to return to his homeland. On the way home, he has a confrontation with Laban and makes an interesting statement. Jacob said, "If the God of my father, the God of Abraham and the Fear of Isaac, had not been on my side, surely now you would have sent me away empty-handed. God saw my affliction and the labor of my hands and rebuked you last night" (Genesis 31:42).

After 20 years of hard labor, Jacob expected to be sent away with something to show for it. Yet the Black community in this nation labored as slaves for 250 years and again under harsh social, political and economic oppression for another 100 years, and what do they have to show for their endless, backbreaking labor and toil?

According to the Institute for Policy Studies report "Dreams Deferred," the median wealth for Black families in 2019 (exactly 400 years after the first African slaves landed on American soil) is $3,600, a mere two percent of the $147,000 owned by White families and roughly half of the $6,600 owned by Hispanic families. Today, 37 percent of Black households own zero or negative wealth, which means that they are literally "empty-handed" (or worse). Although our perception is that great progress has been made toward racial economic equality, the numbers speak for themselves.

In the end, the vision of a new day cast during the Civil Rights Movement never fully dawned for the Black community as a whole. I asked a friend on the Eastside who grew up during the tail end of Jim Crow how different life was on the other side of Civil Rights. "It didn't change like they said it would," he told me. I could feel the disappointment in his voice. Much like the demoralizing and abrupt end of Reconstruction, the Civil Rights era too went out with a whimper instead of a bang.

CHAPTER FOUR

ANGELIC VISITATION

AFTER THE CLOSE OF the tent revival, we announced to our church that we needed leaders for a new Bible study. There were eight little girls, ages eight to ten, who had just been baptized, and we knew that we needed to help them grow in their newfound faith. Two other couples who had frequented the tent and who had gotten to know the girls volunteered to help us, and we started a small ministry that later became the Kingdom Club.

We decided that in order to fully embrace these precious children whom God had sent into our lives, we would do best to bring them into our homes. We wanted to show them what a life devoted to God and to Jesus Christ looked like in the context of everyday family life. And since not a single one of the girls had a married father and mother, we wanted to show them the love, safety and protection that a nuclear family can provide in order to give them vision for their own families one day.

Our initial idea was to split up the girls and to have two or three at each of our homes to allow us to get to know them individually and to share with them in a more intimate setting. We set a time and met at the park right across the street from the projects where most of the girls lived. Two of the girls saw us coming and ran to our cars just like they had done upon our arrival every night of the tent revival. Then they immediately scurried off to get the other girls and soon returned with four more girls in tow.

The six girls present informed us that two of the girls, a set of identical twins named Tierra and Trinity, had moved out of the neighborhood since the tent revival and had not been seen since. We tried the number we had for them, but we could not reach them and since they attended a different school than the rest of the girls, we had no way to get in touch with them.

We split the girls up between the three couples and each headed off to our respective homes. We quickly discovered, though, that the girls missed each other and that they spent most of the time asking what the others were doing. So instead, we decided to keep the group intact and rotate from house to house. Since we had three children under the age of two at our house, we all met in the home of our dear friends, Nancy and Sean Johnson, for dinner and Bible study.

Nancy and Sean, without any real forethought, prepared one of their family's favorite meals—taco salad—which the girls liked so much that we have literally never changed the menu since. Whenever we would talk about serving something different, they would dig in their heels and petition us for taco salad. One of the first things we noticed with the girls was their poor eating habits. Not only did they eat a lot of junk food and very few fruits and vegetables, they also did not have regular meal times aside from school breakfast and lunch.

It did not occur to me until several nights after meeting the girls how long the girls were staying at the tent each night and how late it must be for elementary school students. These were fourth, fifth and sixth graders staying out until nine o'clock and later on school nights. I wondered where their parents were and what was going on at home for them to all be out so late.

I soon discovered that most of the girls lived with single mothers who often worked late to make the ends meet. When the girls got home from school, usually there was an older sister to greet them, but sometimes there wasn't anyone. So they roamed the streets until dark and did pretty much whatever they wanted to do, to include staying sometimes to the bitter end of the tent revival.

The other couple who agreed to help us start our Bible study was then mayoral candidate (and now at the writing of this book, mayor of Charleston), John Tecklenburg, and his wife Sandy. The second week of our scheduled Thursday meetings, no one else was able to attend, so they brought all of the girls into their home for dinner and Bible study and to sing hymns with John, who is a gifted pianist and singer.

At one point during the evening, one of the girls named Taliyah was walking down the hall when she let out a shriek that made everyone's hair stand on end. She ran to meet the rest of the group, and when they questioned her, she told them that there was a large shining man in one of the rooms. They all went to investigate and found nothing but an empty guest bedroom.

John and Sandy tried to calm her down and explain that what she had seen was an angel and that this was not completely uncommon. Both the Old and New Testaments are sprinkled with angelic visitations. From Abraham to Mary to Cornelius, encounters with large shining men have driven the narrative of the Bible at many critical junctures. And one thing they always seem to say is, "Do not be afraid!"

Despite the reassurance, Taliyah was clearly spooked and almost inconsolable. When I spoke with her the following week, she still wasn't ready to talk about it. I wondered if it was one of the angels who had filled our empty chairs each night in the tent. I guess, like Latoyah, we had taken his church down too and he needed a place to go.

Either way, we knew that God was blessing our step of faith to take on these precious girls and that we were on the right track. And we knew that we needed all of the angels we could get.

Emanuel Nine

On the morning of June 18, 2015, I awoke to a tragic series of text messages from friends informing me of a shooting at a historic Black church less than three miles from my home and less than one mile from the Eastside neighborhood. I immediately began to read the accounts of what we all know now as Emanuel Nine, a horrible massacre initiated by a White gunman named Dylann Roof who opened fire during a Wednesday night Bible study in a Black church in hopes of starting, in his own words, "a race war."

This incident came just two months after an unarmed Black man named Walter Scott had been gunned down by a White police officer after a routine traffic stop in North Charleston. Amazingly, the Walter Scott tragedy had not incited any riots or unrest locally as the bold and unwavering forgiveness of his mother and other family members doused any flames of hatred and division which might otherwise have been kindled. But this—nine innocent people murdered in cold blood, in a church no less—was a whole different story.

Since Thursday was the day we regularly met for our Bible study with the girls, I decided to call each of the parents to make sure everyone was alright and to let them know that Bible study would be canceled. At the time, the murderer was still at large which incited a tremendous amount of fear throughout the entire community, and rightly so.

The first parent I got on the phone was a single mom who I had baptized at the tent revival along with her children. The fear in her voice was tangible as she began to share her heart's desire to get out of the neighborhood for good. She loved her children and lived for them, and her concern for their safety was a burden she carried every day. This was the last straw for her, and she was already beginning to make plans to move up to Philadelphia where she had some family.

As the community woke up to the news of the Emanuel shooting, prayer vigils began to pop up all over the city. Rather than the violence which broke out in cities all over the nation such as Ferguson and Baltimore following similar incidents, the city of Charleston had a strange peace that seemed to hover over downtown and the surrounding areas.

After making all of my phone calls, I rushed out of the house to attend a prayer meeting at Morris Brown AME, a sister church to Emanuel AME, and by the time I got there, the church was overflowing and the street in front of the church was packed from sidewalk to sidewalk with folks, Black and White, young and old, who were praying for the community. As they prayed in the church, we prayed on the street as a local minister facilitated the intercession.

That night, my wife and I attended another prayer vigil at a church around the corner which ended with a walk down to Mother Emanuel where each us laid a white lily at the front entrance of the church. A month later, we led a prayer group to the same spot in front of the church where a beautiful memorial had been erected to the victims, and we washed the feet of Black visitors from all over the country who were paying their respects, asking for forgiveness and praying for racial reconciliation.

The prayer meetings and rallies were so numerous that you couldn't attend or even keep up with them all. Rather than erupting in violence, the city erupted in prayer, unity and compassion for those who had lost their lives as well as for the family members and friends who were left behind.

A miraculous outflow of forgiveness from family, church and

community members began to flow forth, seemingly washing out the tide of violence and hatred that tried to take root. A hate group scheduled a rally downtown and attempted to stir up the crowd into anger and aggression, but their shouts were only dampened by the peace hanging in the atmosphere and no riot formed.

Tens of thousands of people gathered just days after the tragedy on Sunday morning to form a human chain across the Ravenel Bridge, which connects downtown Charleston to Mount Pleasant, to visibly display unity in the city. The scene was surreal. The outpouring of love between the Black community and the White community in a historically divided city incited hope, not just for the city, but for the entire nation and even around the world.

Pain and Rejection

Despite the incredible response from the victims' families and the community at large, a mass murder by a White assailant in a historic Black church instantly conjured up images from the Civil Rights era and beyond that many in our nation longed to forget. During Civil Rights, violent attacks against Black churches were a common form of intimidation that became a symbolic act of resistance by the Southern White community to fight the termination of Jim Crow.

When I look at a guy like Dylann Roof, I can't help but ask the question of how our society produced an individual with so much hatred in his heart toward people who have more melanin in their skin than he does. It was shocking to watch his unflinching conviction that he had done the right thing and that there was no need to repent for his course of action in ruthlessly taking nine innocent lives.

ANGELIC VISITATION

Yet should we be totally surprised by the existence of such an individual? In order to understand Dylann Roof, we must be willing to confront the pervasive mindset that existed almost exclusively throughout our entire nation for centuries about black and brown skinned people. An entire philosophy and even theology was crafted around the premise that people of color were inherently inferior to White people. This notion became so rooted in the thought life of the American people that it undergirded every facet of our formation as a country and the development of our society in the first several centuries of our nationhood.

Black inferiority was not a hidden thread woven subtly through the fabric of society, it was publically illustrated in more ways than we could ever imagine today. Awful caricatures of Black men and women depicting them as stupid, lazy, aggressive, ugly and servile appeared in every facet of American culture from signs and billboards to cereal boxes and syrup containers to books, theatre and later television.

The name Jim Crow came from a Black character in the blackface theatre depicted as a dimwitted yet amiable buffoon who didn't know his right from his left. This was the image of Blackness that the parents and grandparents and great grandparents of Dylan Roof's generation grew up with. Since few Whites actually knew any Black people intimately, this is how they were thought of and perceived by the vast majority of the culture.

Nearly 200 years after the penning of the United States Constitution, Martin Luther King, Jr. stood on the steps of the Lincoln Memorial in Washington DC and spoke to a crowd of over a quarter of a million people gathered for the 1963 March on Washington. "I have a dream that one day this nation will rise up and live out the true meaning of its creed: 'We hold these truths to be self-evident: that all men are created equal.'"

I honor the fact that the Constitution is considered by many to be holy ground (and it is not my heart to tread on anyone's sacred space just for the sake of it), yet from its very inception there is a clear disconnect in the language which found its way onto that celebrated parchment and its application in real, everyday life. Growing up as a White kid in an affluent neighborhood, I did not have eyes to see it. But I can assure you that every single Black person standing in the crowd that fateful day listening to Dr. King knew it all too well.

What they knew was the great unspoken American secret that the phrase, "all men," did not in practice ever actually refer to "all men." Nor was it intended to. Those two little words were a code of sorts, an abbreviated and covert way of saying, "all White men of European descent." Black men of African descent, particularly the hundreds of thousands of them who were enslaved at the time of our nation's birth, unquestionably did not possess any share in the "unalienable" Constitutional rights of "liberty" or "the pursuit of happiness."

What was so remarkable about the moment in which Dr. King stood and delivered his "I Have a Dream" Speech was his ability to bring to light a 200 year old thread of hypocrisy which had been woven into the very fabric of our nation. Both Native and African Americans had known it long before the words of the Constitution were ever written, but throughout the Civil Rights struggle, the eyes of more and more people in the mainstream culture were opened as they became keenly aware that something was amiss from the very start in America.

The fundamental problem with hypocrisy is that one has no ability to see it while they are in it. Sadly, it took White America hundreds of years to figure out that our enslavement of both Native Americans and Africans was morally wrong and another hundred years to come to the same conclusion about institutional segregation. Even then, it took decades more before some were ready to admit it.

Angelic Visitation

The United States government in 2008 issued a formal apology for the periods of slavery and Jim Crow and in 2009 made an admission of guilt regarding the Native American people, although the latter included a clause denying any and all liability associated with the statement making it read more like legal jargon than a heartfelt act of contrition. And interestingly enough, the Charleston City Council narrowly passed (by a 7-5 vote) a resolution to apologize for our city's role in slavery during the writing of this book in 2018. Yet while it took our government centuries to recognize it, I can assure you that the hypocrisy was not lost for a moment on Native and African Americans.

As Dr. King was shedding light on this hidden undercurrent of American history, you can hear the voices of agreement rising up from the crowd. They knew it all along. Who could hide the hypocrisy of daily American life from those who had experienced the dark side of it firsthand? It was written on every foundation and every pillar of our culture from the smallest social interaction to the greatest halls of government. They cheered and applauded not because they were hearing something new, but because an ancient leviathan was being brought to light in front of the entire nation.

The sad reality is that 50 short years ago, the Dylann Roofs of this world were not only tolerated in our nation, they were celebrated and embraced by the mainstream White community as defenders of the American social order. And what's worse, they were usually protected with total immunity by local law enforcement, particularly in the South.

This includes members of the KKK and other White supremacist organizations who committed acts of violence and terror (and who were often prominent members of the community) as well as politicians who used the united Southern Democratic party (which faced no political opposition due to the violent suppression of the

Black vote) to ensure that the White powers that be remained unshaken for as long as humanly possible south of the Mason Dixon line.

It's easy to point the finger at the men who wrote the laws and the men who wore the hoods in order to terrorize the Black community into submission and compliance, but it was the silence of the masses—business men and women, stay-at-home parents and grandparents, teachers and shop keepers, common every day members of society—which gave tacit approval to the violence, the terror and to the overarching societal structure that held it all in place.

The philosophy of race inferiority is embedded in the DNA of the United States, and it didn't simply go away with the advent of Civil Rights. Rather, it was driven underground, out of the mainstream and away from the public eye. Despite our politically correct culture and the carefully orchestrated diversity that we see every day in entertainment, media and advertizing, racism is unfortunately alive and well in America today.

In hindsight, we must be willing to boldly acknowledge the blatant and horrific nature of our error and recognize it for what it is. White people of European decent as the dominant race in America intentionally, systematically and unequivocally elevated one race over another and built an entire culture around the presumption that the more melanin you have in your skin, the more inferior you are as a human being.

Even within the Black community, this twisted racial psychology became deeply rooted and has survived as a stronghold that divides family, friends and neighbors based on their skin tone. A neighbor of mine shared her experience in a Black sorority and the "brown bag test" they used to determine eligibility for membership. If your skin was darker than a brown paper bag, you were out. If it was lighter, you were in. Just as slaves were commonly separated based on their pigmentation and given preferential treatment for having lighter skin, Black individuals with very dark skin are likely to face more prejudice in their own communities to this day, sometimes blatantly and other times subconsciously.

The peculiar thing about the great American error of skin tone inferiority is that it was birthed out of the economic institution of slavery rather than vice versa. Long before any Africans were enslaved on American soil, tens of thousands of Natives were enslaved here, some of whom were exported to the Caribbean and some of whom remained in the Colonies. The problem as mentioned previously with Native American slaves was that they were more susceptible to European contagious diseases and they escaped more easily due to their familiarity with the lay of the land. As a result, they did not prove to be the economic powerhouse that African slaves were.

But just imagine if Native American slaves had been as productive as African slaves proved to be. There may have been no need to import Africans to North America, and the transatlantic slave trade may have never even materialized. In that case, would our modern day struggle for Civil Rights be for Native Americans rather than African Americans?

My point is that slavery itself, the sheer exertion of force of one people group over another, is what bred and nurtured the pervasive belief that African skin is inferior to European skin. This phenomenon happened all throughout the British Empire, but the sheer number of slaves who were imported to America and later birthed on American soil intensified the situation here.

There is a saying that is attributed to Thomas Cranmer, a leader of the Protestant Reformation, which explains how human beings come to chose and ultimately justify our actions. "What the heart desires, the will chooses and the mind justifies." The reason for desiring and choosing to implement slavery in America is obvious—it was extremely profitable economically. Yet the way we justified it as a society is the real tragedy of the American tale.

The White Church

WHILE REHASHING AMERICAN HISTORY through the lens of race relations is painful and difficult, there is one aspect of our national narrative which grieves me more than all of the rest combined. Slavery and oppression are as common throughout world history as sand is on the seashore. In fact, there are more people enslaved today than at any other time in world history. I am not shocked by evil—although I am grieved by it—because I understand the fallen nature of man and the brokenness of our world. But what shocks me to the core about the American story is the role of the White church in justifying and condoning both slavery and Jim Crow.

Please note that when I refer to the White church (or to the Black church), I am not referring to a building or to a Sunday morning worship service or to a group of ordained leaders, but rather to the entire body of believers who call themselves Christ-followers. The Greek word used for "church" in the New Testament is ecclesia, which literally means an assembly of people. Of course, the leaders and the buildings and the services are all important aspects of church culture, but they are not the church. The people of God are the church.

Also, while I do not like making a distinction between the White church and the Black church, I do so for reference only. God does not see color and his true church is not divided by race or ethnicity or any other earthly marker. Yet sadly, the church in America is starkly

Angelic Visitation

divided by Black and White, and it has been for 400 years. So when I refer to the White church or to the Black church, I do so with sadness in my heart hoping that one day there will be no such thing.

All throughout the two dark eras of slavery and institutionalized segregation, the White church in America played a devastating, primary role in encouraging rather than opposing and contesting the violent oppression of Black people. Rather than being convicted by the preaching and teaching of the church, White slave owners and non-slave owners alike were comforted that their position was both Biblical and in alignment with God's heart and will. An entire theology was built around the social philosophy that Black people are inherently inferior to Whites.

For hundreds of years, the message was preached from the pulpits of America and upheld as theological truth that all Africans descended from Ham, Noah's son whose descendents he cursed following the flood, and that slavery was their resulting punishment from God. Volumes upon volumes of work were written and published based on this single scripture using very thin evidence to back up this twisted theological position.

Many prominent ministers and lay people alike believed and preached that Africans were so degenerate that they could not function outside of the bonds of slavery and that slavery was actually a saving grace for Blacks because they would not be able to live in a civilized society otherwise. In essence, slavery was their God-ordained place in the culture and to set them free would be to doom them to utter failure.

Many other scriptures were used to defend slavery and Jim Crow as well as the enslavement, massacre and displacement of the Native American people. American defenders of slavery nearly always used Biblical justification for their position, creating a moral appeal for the institution of slavery based on scripture.

Yet as the American era of slavery came to a close following the Civil War, the scriptures condoning slavery faded away into the annuls of history, and the curse of Ham became the primary theological pillar of racist thought which spilled over into the era of Jim Crow. Other Biblical passages such as the dispersion following the Tower of Babel were also cited to demonstrate God's intention to separate the races and to keep them from intermixing.

The concept of God-ordained White superiority and racial separatism, as backward as it may sound to us today, explains why nearly all White churches in the South, as well as many in the North, stood against emancipation and later integration. Just like any effective propaganda, the message was repeated and repeated and repeated until it was hammered into the minds of White people from their earliest childhood on, becoming cemented as an undeniable fact.

This is very important for us to remember in order to avoid falling into the trap of human judgment. The point here is not to vilify White people or anyone else for that matter, but rather to expose a lie from the enemy which was embraced and accepted as truth not just by unbelievers, but by those in the church who called themselves followers of Jesus Christ, a man whose stated purpose in ministry was "to preach good news to the poor" and "to set the captives free" (Isaiah 61:1).

White people who lived in the era of slavery and Jim Crow are no different than White people living in America today or any other people group living anywhere else in the world at any other time in history. Every human being who has ever walked the earth shares the same sin nature which corrupted humanity at the fall.

Unfortunately, because of a wrong belief system, the White Christians who lived during these two periods of our history were unable to wholly embrace and fulfill the royal law of love, Jesus' great commandment to love God and to love our neighbor as ourselves. Instead, the message of American Christianity from its very inception was to love your White neighbor as yourself, while denigrating Africans as property and Native Americans as heathens.

While this mindset is almost impossible for us to imagine in our modern context, again we must guard our hearts from judgment. When you grow up and live in a certain framework your entire life that is never even remotely challenged by anyone in your sphere of influence, it is extremely difficult for an individual to break out of the mold and arrive at a different conclusion than that which has been spoon-fed to them since birth.

I have a good friend in his 70s who was born during Jim Crow and who never met a Black person until he went to college at age 18. As a child, his parents took him to blackface performances, which were a staple during the Jim Crow era and which indelibly shaped his perception of Black people long before he ever met one. Was his mindset about the Black community completely wrong? Of course. But I would contend that it would be equally wrong to judge him for his ignorance. Fortunately, he realized upon meeting and getting to know Black people for himself that they are inherently no different than White people or any other race, and he went on to become a minister who fights to this day for racial reconciliation, particularly in the church.

I believe it is also important for us to remember and acknowledge that White Americans are not the only ones who have fallen into a trap of pervasive, cultural-wide, institutional racism. Some prevalent modern examples are Nazi Germany and Rwanda, where manipulated cultural divides resulted in hatred to the point of mass murder.

Even God's chosen people, the nation of Israel, fell into the trap of a national, all-encompassing racist mindset toward the Samaritans. Jesus exposed and warred against this cultural stronghold through his interaction with the Samaritan woman at the well and also in his parable of the Good Samaritan.

Were his disciples wrong to be shocked by these two targeted attacks against their way of thinking in which they had been raised and led to believe all of their lives? Hardly. Yet God was merciful to expose it to them and to give them a chance to repent and change their minds in order to embrace a people group whom God loved just as much as he loved them or anyone else on the face of the planet.

In the same way, God in his mercy began to expose the strongholds of slavery and racism toward Black people in the White church during the Second Great Awakening beginning in the late eighteenth century and carrying over into the middle of the nineteenth century leading all the way up to the Civil War. Christians primarily in the North became convicted of the gross sin of chattel slavery, and a strong abolition movement arose chiefly out of Northern churches.

Yet despite the momentum of the Christian abolition movement in the North, it did not make a dent in the theology of the church in the South. Persisting through the Civil War and for an entire century to follow, Southern Christians held fast to their separationist ideology and upheld the belief system of White superiority which enabled and undergirded Jim Crow.

The Northern states were certainly not exempt from segregation and the intentional exclusion of Black people from mainstream society during the 100 years between the Civil War and the end of the Civil Rights Movement, but because of the voice of the church boldly speaking out against slavery and racism, no blanket system of segregation such as Jim Crow was allowed to take root above the Mason-Dixon Line.

Instead, segregation in the North was accomplished on the local level, less overtly than in the South. Many like to think of the post-

Angelic Visitation

Civil War North as a safe haven for Blacks seeking a better life and as a refuge from Jim Crow oppression, yet segregation and institutional racism were still just as much a part of everyday life in the North as they were in the South with schools, restaurants, theatres and whole neighborhoods divided by skin color. Segregation was not a distinctly Southern problem—it was an American problem.

In the concluding scene of the 1915 film, *The Birth of a Nation*, the Ku Klux Klan is depicted as rescuing a White family from barbaric looking Black renegades who are trying to break into their home and murder them in cold blood. At the last moment, the Klan charges in on horseback wearing their white robes and hoods to rescue the White victims from the vicious attack of the Negro mob, thus restoring order to a small town under siege. The Klan members then disarm and chase off the Black assailants, who flee in a panic, and they hold a parade through the streets of the city to celebrate their victory.

The film then shifts to two quick scenes that cap the narration: the first of hell and the second of heaven. What is shocking and also telling about the film's portrayal of heaven is that there are no people of color there, only a bunch of very White folks celebrating under the image of a very White Jesus who is holding out his hands and welcoming the crowd into his eternal kingdom.

This homogenous picture of heaven stands in direct contrast to the one provided in the book of Revelation, which describes a great multitude wearing white robes and standing before the throne of God "from every nation, from all tribes and peoples and languages" (Revelation 7:9). To depict Blacks as ignorant and malicious and aggressive toward White women is one thing, but to insinuate that they will be excluded entirely from the courts of heaven is a whole different statement.

Despite protest from the NAACP and other like organizations, the overtly racist film enjoyed great commercial success at the box office. The racist underpinnings of America, from Hollywood to the Deep South, can clearly be seen in the overwhelmingly positive response to a film which features White actors in blackface, Black people as deplorable buffoons and which puts a positive spin on the brutal lynching of a Black man. The KKK immediately saw a surge in membership following the film's release and used it as a recruitment tool all the way up to the 1970s. When the American Film Institute released its list of the 100 best films of all time in 1998, The Birth of a Nation ranked 44th.

Again, what is shocking and grievous to me about the film is not its shameless promotion of anti-Black racist sentiment. The entire culture at the time was saturated with an enveloping mixture of blatant anti-Black policy and propaganda. But the giant leap from making a racist social statement to making a theological one should send up red flags for any believer.

To equate salvation with Whiteness or any other racial or cultural marker is one of the most heinous theological errors we can possibly make as followers of Jesus Christ. It flies directly in the face of scripture, but even more so, it completely misses the heart of God. God loves all of his children the same regardless of where we are born or how much melanin we have in our skin. In the eyes of the Lord, we are all equally precious and beautiful. As Paul wrote to the Galatians, "There is neither Jew nor Greek, there is neither slave nor free, there is no male and female, for you are all one in Christ Jesus" (Galatians 3:28).

Yet as generation after generation grew up in a world where White was good and Black was bad, White Christians all over America from sea to shining sea became trapped in a mindset and a cultural stronghold which prevented them from seeing all people and races as "one in Christ Jesus." And in order to understand the depth of the root of racism in the American church, we must look all the way back to her inception. Truly, racism is a disease that has plagued the White church in America from her first interaction with the New World.

THE GREAT AMERICAN DISCONNECT

IT IS CLEAR FROM the charters and the historical accounts which document the founding of the American colonies from the very first settlements onward that both the practice and the advancement of the Christian faith were major motivating factors in establishing the New World. The vast majority of our founding fathers were pious and religious men who gave their Christian faith the utmost priority both in their individual lives as well as in the life of their communities.

In fact, many Europeans who came to the colonial United States saw it as the Promised Land, a refuge and safe haven from the religious persecution roaring across the mother continent as a result of the Protestant Reformation. When our founding fathers were considering the Great Seal of America, one of the images proposed was that of Moses leading the children of Israel across the Red Sea, out of Egyptian bondage and into the land flowing with milk and honey.

But at the very same time, there is a blatant disconnect beginning with the very first explorers and settlers who landed on our shores between religious devotion and adherence to Jesus' golden rule, to "do to others what you would have them do to you" (Matthew 7:12, NIV), not to mention the second half of his great commandment, to "love your neighbor as yourself" (Mark 12:31, NIV).

Despite sailing under a Christian charter and holding regular Christian devotions with his crew, Christopher Columbus clearly had a different primary motive than sharing the good news of Jesus

Christ with new people groups. The actions of Columbus and his men to kill and enslave rather than convert and baptize the Natives reveal that the Christian language in his charter was nothing more than a thin veil over an imperialistic and capitalistic enterprise to expand the Spanish Empire and to provide his backers with a return on their investment.

Columbus was not alone. The atrocities committed against the indigenous people in the West Indies and all across the Americas were almost all perpetrated under Christian evangelical charters. Claiming to follow a man who practiced nonviolence and who told his disciples that "those who live by the sword, die by the sword" (Matthew 26:52), the violent and underhanded actions of the earliest North American settlers toward indigenous peoples casts a dark shadow over our nation's Christian heritage, which may have been flawless in word but not in deed.

Although some true missionaries, such as David Brainerd, did devote their lives to sharing the gospel with the Native people they encountered on North American soil (often living among the tribes they sought to convert), their witness was vastly hindered by the staggering numbers of Native Americans who were murdered, enslaved and displaced by European colonists.

In 1637, a "Day of Thanksgiving" was declared by the governor of the Massachusetts Bay Colony after 700 unarmed men, women and children of the Pequot Tribe were brutally murdered in an early dawn raid. Many of the surviving Pequot men and boys were then captured and shipped to the Caribbean as slaves. This violent massacre was perpetrated by the inhabitants of a Puritan colony where missing church on Sunday morning was a punishable offense and where every single inhabitant would have sworn allegiance to the Prince of Peace.

The attack on the Pequot tribe occurred just 15 years after the autumn harvest feast shared by Plymouth colonists and Wampanoag Indians, which many historians believe to be the basis for the Thanksgiving holiday we celebrate to this day. The two contrasting stories illustrate the checkered history of the American colonies in regard to the Native people and explain why protestors gather each year on Thanksgiving Day at Plymouth Rock to commemorate a "National Day of Mourning," in order to shed light on the traditional Thanksgiving narrative presented in grade school text books which glosses over the millions of Native Americans who lost their lives as a direct result of brutal European colonization.

As African slaves were being imported throughout the American colonial period, Native American slaves were being exported in incredible numbers. The brutality of American chattel slavery for both Native Americans and Africans as well as the horrific transport of slaves both coming to and leaving from American soil is well-documented. No one alive at the time would have been able to claim ignorance of the conditions of these poor human souls, and the entire culture profited from their brutal oppression.

The displacement of the Native people from their land is also a tragic aspect of the story, from the very first arrival of European settlers to the government-mandated removal of around 50,000 Native Americans in 1830, which forced men, women and children to walk 2,200 miles to Indian Territory in modern-day Oklahoma, a horrific ordeal we all know today as the Trail of Tears.

So despite what was written on paper about the Christian impetus for European exploration and settlement of the New World (and despite the extreme religious devotion of a large portion of early explorers and colonists), it is painfully obvious that there were higher priorities at work in the founding of colonial America than the quest for religious freedom as the oversimplified grade-school narrative describes.

The reality is that many of the English settlers who risked their lives to traverse the Atlantic Ocean to come to America were poor and had no ability to own land or create wealth back at home. In much of European culture, land ownership directly correlated with one's net worth and therefore their status in society. Many English companies offered land as a way to motivate colonists to attempt the dangerous voyage across the Atlantic. Coming to America represented a doorway to a better life and provided a chance to improve one's social status and cultural standing.

The problem with this rudimentary version of the American Dream is that Europeans and Native Americans had completely opposite understandings of how land was owned and controlled. Native Americans believed that you couldn't own land any more than you could own the ocean or the sky. They lived on the land and used the land for hunting, fishing and farming, but they never saw their inhabitation of any particular piece of land as permanent.

When English settlers began to "own" property, erect fences and drive out the Native people from land they had utilized for centuries (and in some cases, millennia), a major clash of cultures ensued. In the early days when the population of settlers was still sparse, peace treaties were often successfully negotiated and functioned in some places to maintain harmony between English colonists and Native tribes.

But as the sheer number of English colonists increased over time seeking the opportunity to become land owners themselves, the more it became clear that peace treaties were not a viable long-term option. Death, enslavement and displacement prevailed as the colonial solution to the Native American problem.

Among these three options, enslavement had a two-fold appeal both as a way to seize the land and as a vehicle for wealth creation. As opposed to African slaves, whom colonists had to pay vast sums to import, Native American slaves represented a way to actually generate capital. Tens of thousands of Native American slaves were captured and exported from the colonies, funding much of the importation of African slaves, who performed better overall on American soil.

Timothy writes in his first letter, "The law is for people who are sexually immoral, or who practice homosexuality, or are slave traders, liars, promise breakers, or who do anything else that contradicts the wholesome teaching" (1 Timothy 1:10, NLT). Another translation used for slaver traders is "enslavers" or "those who take someone captive in order to sell him into slavery" (ESV footnote).

According to Timothy, taking someone captive and selling them into slavery "contradicts wholesome teaching." Yes, there was a culture of slavery in ancient Israel and even in the Law of Moses, but Jesus Christ launched an entirely new culture when he came to earth and proclaimed: "Repent, for the kingdom of heaven is at hand" (Matthew 4:17).

Rather than establishing his kingdom by violent force, Jesus submitted to the wicked forceful hand of his earthly rulers and built his eternal kingdom through obedience to his Father's will, non-violent surrender to the earthly powers that be, and a gospel of unconditional love and forgiveness. His last act before leaving the world was to send out his disciples to proclaim good news to the ends of the earth, to share the gospel with all of the people groups on the planet who had not yet heard of his wonderful offer of eternal life, which he bought and paid for with his own blood.

The Great Commission is a clear mandate from God to give away the free gift of salvation which we have received as followers of Jesus Christ. The concept of going somewhere, to a new land and a new people group, and taking their land or God-forbid taking their very lives through murder or enslavement, all for the means of personal gain, stands in direct opposition to the heart of the great commission and the gospel of the Kingdom. Yet this is exactly what European settlers did on American soil and called it Christianity. No wonder they didn't win many Native American converts.

First John 4:20 says that "he who does not love his brother whom he has seen cannot love God whom he has not seen." Jesus told his disciples that love would be the unmistakable and distinguishing mark of their lives. "Your love for one another will prove to the world that you are my disciples." (John 13:35, NLT). As the old song goes, "They will know we are Christians by our love, by our love." The disconnect between religious devotion and the love of Jesus Christ in early American culture with regard to Native and African Americans is staggering. Where is the love that Jesus so adamantly taught and demonstrated both through his words and his very life?

Were the earliest American settlers devout followers of Jesus Christ? Did they attend church and read their Bibles and pray and fast and tithe and keep the Sabbath? The answer is a resounding yes—and probably far more faithfully than most of us could claim today. Additionally, nearly all educational institutions from elementary schools to universities were run by Christian denominations, and the influence of Christian faith and values could not be denied at any level of society from government to business to entertainment.

Yet in the midst of it all, where is the simple humanity to treat a fellow human being who happened to be born into a different ethnic group with the most basic dignity and respect? It is precisely here that we see the great American disconnect. Utterly committed to religious devotion and to dutifully observing Christian tradition, the earliest American settlers could not see the image of God in their fellow human beings of Native American and African descent—and therefore they were unable to accept and embrace them according to Jesus' greatest and most basic commandment to love.

FREE EXERCISE OF RELIGION?

FROM OUR VERY FIRST YEARS of kindergarten and primary school, American children are taught the narrative of our earliest settlers escaping religious persecution in England and across Europe to worship God freely on American soil. The free exercise of religion and the liberty to worship in whatever manner we choose has been and continues to be touted as one of our highest and most noble virtues as a nation.

The First Amendment to the Constitution, which was ratified in 1791, states that "Congress shall make no law respecting an establishment of religion, or prohibiting the free exercise thereof; or abridging the freedom of speech, or of the press; or the right of the people peaceably to assemble, and to petition the Government for a redress of grievances."

The fact that this Amendment serves as the opening statement of the Bill of Rights clearly indicates the high priority placed on our ability to assemble and worship God freely. Yet in light of this language, one of the most ironic aspects of the history of the White church is our utter hypocrisy concerning religious freedom.

From the early 1600s, White Christians fervently suppressed the worship of African slaves during the epoch of institutional slavery and later viciously persecuted the Black church during Jim Crow (Native American religion was likewise targeted and repressed).

Slave owners were so suspicious of their slaves that they rarely allowed them to congregate for any reason, religious or otherwise, without a White person present. Slave preachers were closely watched by White overseers and had to be careful what they said, both in and out of church. Due to White surveillance, they were forced to preach a gospel that aligned with White theology, which strongly emphasized submission within the master-slave relationship and the importance of complete obedience in every situation, no questions asked.

Only in underground meetings and secret gatherings were Black preachers allowed to truly share their hearts and express what they believed about the nature of God deep down in their souls. Drums, which were a staple of African music, culture and worship, were banned in church altogether creating an even greater need for secret meetings in order to achieve a full expression of worship among African slaves.

Often, slaves were forced to join their masters for worship in their White churches, where they were made to sit in the "negro pew," the section set apart for Black people. Even when slaves were converted to Christianity and became professing believers in Christ, they were still forced to sit away from the White congregation in separate seating, often a gallery or balcony which was out of sight of the White church-goers.

Following the Civil War, Black churches became the target of much White violence due to their tendency to house activist movements. Bombings of Black churches were a weekly occurrence during the height of Jim Crow, and even in the half-century since, we have continued to see violent attacks persisting against the Black church.

In a parallel but strikingly similar storyline, Native American religion was also violently suppressed by the church and actually outlawed officially by Congress in 1883 with the passing of the "Rules for Indian Courts." These policies banned many Native religious customs to include Native dances and the practice of medicine men, which were seen as major threats to Native American assimilation into White culture. Although the ban was weakened due to a policy shift in the 1930s, it was not until the passage of the American Indian Religious Freedom Act (AIRFA) in 1978 that Native Americans regained their legal right to worship God freely on United States soil.

Additionally, many Native American children were forcibly taken from their families and made to attend Christian boarding schools, known as Indian Residential Schools, in order to assimilate them into Euro-American Christian culture. The schools used cultural immersion to "civilize" Native American children, forbidding them to speak their native languages and even replacing their names with European ones. The highly controversial Indian Child Welfare Act, likewise passed in 1978, finally gave Native American parents the legal right to deny the placement of their children in off-reservation schools.

The irony of religious suppression in the land of the free is not difficult to see. Martin Luther King, Jr. famously wrote in his Letter from a Birmingham Jail, "Injustice anywhere is a threat to justice everywhere. We are caught in an inescapable network of mutuality, tied in a single garment of destiny. Whatever affects one directly, affects all indirectly."

Rather than preaching the gospel and trusting in God for the results, the White church in America has sought conversion and assimilation, both with Native and Black Americans, through force rather than love. Sadly, our track record in this matter sides us with those who suppressed and murdered Jesus—in an attempt to protect the people from false religion—rather than Jesus himself.

The Religious Spirit

When Jesus Christ walked the earth, his primary opposition and ultimately the movement that arose to orchestrate his brutal murder came from the most revered religious leaders of his day. Today, we have been conditioned to read the words "Pharisee" or "Sadducee" with a snarl on our lips, but in Jesus' culture, these were the most highly respected people in the entire societal hierarchy. Not only were they esteemed religious leaders, they also served a political and judicial function, which would have made them like a cross between a senator, a judge and a senior pastor. These guys were honored, admired and revered by all.

Yet it was this very faction of men who conspired against and crucified the God of the Universe when he graced the earth in human form. They were so consumed with their system of religious devotion that they could not recognize the very love of God incarnate. Rather than celebrating the life-giving, healing miracles of Jesus, again and again these religious leaders hardened their heart toward him and continually schemed together how they were going to destroy him.

When confronting these religious leaders just before his death, Jesus said to them: "Woe to you, scribes and Pharisees, hypocrites! For you tithe mint and dill and cumin, and have neglected the weightier matters of the law: justice and mercy and faithfulness. These you ought to have done, without neglecting the others" (Matthew 23:23).

You can almost hear Jesus' voice issuing a strikingly similar indictment against the early American church: "You perform and hold fast to your religious devotion, yet you kill and enslave and displace innocent human beings all under the banner of the Christian faith. You should have taken care of them first and then committed yourself to the practice of religion."

This same thought could be carried forward into the periods of African slavery and Jim Crow, and yes, even into our day. "You pray morning and night, but you rape your female slaves and sell your

Angelic Visitation

offspring into perpetual slavery. You read your Bible every day, yet you target and murder innocent Black men in the streets, often right after church on Sunday afternoon. You go to church every Sunday, but you drive past the projects and step over the homeless man to get there."

This great American disconnect between religious devotion and the simple love of God is fueled by a religious spirit which has led us to believe that showing up to church on Sunday, making the sign of the cross over our chest, praying before our meals, reading the Bible daily and other such religious practices somehow make us right before God.

When I ask people if they know Jesus, one of the most frequent responses I get is, "Yes, I go to church." For centuries, we have equated salvation with church attendance and have bought into the deception that our weekly trip to the church house has some magical power to whitewash all of our wrongdoing from the other six days.

Yet as the prophet Jeremiah warned the people of Israel 600 years before Jesus' birth, attending a religious service in the temple or a church building does not make us right with God. "Do not trust in these deceptive words: 'This is the temple of the LORD, the temple of the LORD, the temple of the LORD.'" (Jeremiah 7:4). What makes us right with God is when we "truly amend [our] ways and [our] deeds" and when we "truly execute justice one with another" (Jeremiah 7:5).

In this system of religious disconnect, Sunday church functions like an obsessive-compulsive cleansing ritual. We have all heard about people who ritually wash their hands five, six or seven times in order to feel clean or those who have to turn the light switch on and off eight, nine or ten times in order to feel safe. The ritual does not actually help the person become clean or safe in reality, but in their mind, it has the power to do so.

In a similar way, the spirit of religion has led us to believe that our church services have the power to make us safe and clean before God. We sit in the same seat, we sing a few songs, we pray a few prayers, we listen to a few scriptures, we may take a lap for communion depending on the tradition, we sing a final song or two, and then when it is all over, we breathe a sigh of relief because the ritual is complete and we feel absolved of our sin.

Yet the reality is that we are not necessarily more or less right with God than when we walked in the front door. We may feel absolved from our sins, and that may be the case if a true transaction of repentance has taken place in our hearts, but the mere act of attending a church service does not actually help our case with God one bit. There is only one way to receive forgiveness for our sins and that is through genuine repentance. To have a priest or pastor speak an absolution over us in a church service means absolutely nothing unless we have had a true heart encounter with God.

We have believed as a culture that we can confess our wrongdoings before God in church and that we are good to go. But confession is only half of repentance. Admitting our sins to God is an important element of repentance, but the root of the word and the core of the concept is to change. Unless we make a commitment in our hearts to change the behavior that we are confessing and to turn away from the wrong we have done, our confession is worthless.

Jesus said that a tree is known by its fruit. A good tree will bear good fruit, and a bad tree will bear bad fruit, period. So when we see violent oppression, murder, enslavement, greed and hypocrisy ruling in the lives of individuals and the culture as a whole, we can be sure that the root of the tree is not healthy regardless of how committed the people are to religious activities.

It is true that salvation only comes through grace by faith in our Lord Jesus Christ. But it is equally true that "faith apart from works is dead" (James 2:26). We can't say to the homeless person on the side of the road, "be warmed and filled without giving them the things needed for the body" (James 2:16). We are not saved by our works, but our works give evidence to our salvation.

A well-known prophet by the name of Bob Jones (no relation to the founder of the university) had a vision of heaven in the 1970s and saw the Lord questioning those who had died and who were facing judgment. According to his vision, the Lord only asked them all just one question. "Did you learn to love?" He didn't ask about their church attendance or their Bible reading plan or their prayer life, he asked about their hearts. I can imagine the question left many deeply religious people dumbfounded and that it will continue to do so until the day of final judgment. Sadly, he shared that the vast majority of the people in the vision had to answer "no" to that heart-penetrating question.

The most tragic outworking of the spirit of religion is that it causes us to miss the forest for the trees. While performing often complicated religious rituals, we miss the very point of it all, which is the simple law of love. And the sad reality is that scores and scores of people in this nation and all over the world have missed heaven because of a false assurance granted to them by their faithful church attendance and religious adherence.

The core of religious deception is that it allows people, both individually and collectively, to feel comfortable in their sin. It is one thing to violently oppress, enslave, displace or murder another human being, but to feel justified in doing so is a very dangerous thing. This is what makes Islam such a terribly malicious force in the world. It is a complicated system of religious devotion that not only justifies but promotes violence and murder. To murder an innocent person is one thing, but to say that God is behind it is entirely another.

Yet the difference between Islamic violence and Christian

violence is night and day. Mohammed both demonstrated violence himself and commanded it in certain instances in the Quran. He was a military leader as well as a religious leader and killed thousands of people in his lifetime. On the other hand, Jesus Christ neither practiced violence nor taught it. Rather than hate and kill your enemies, he taught his followers to love their enemies and to pray for those who mistreat them. Everywhere he went, Jesus healed those who came to him and never inflicted harm on a single soul. After his death, his apostles went forth and did the same, healing the sick, taking care of the poor and even raising the dead back to life.

Rather than inflicting violence on others, Jesus received the violence of the world and did not resist even with a single word. Like a lamb led to the slaughter, he did not lift his voice. When they came at him with swords and clubs, he did not permit Peter to fight back. Instead, he submitted to his own capture, mock trial, false conviction, brutal beating and ultimate murder. Then with his final breath, he released forgiveness, grace and love rather than retaliation and vengeance. Again, his disciples followed suit, laying down their lives to advance the gospel of love.

While it is easy for Islamic extremists to justify violence based on the life of their leader, it is impossible for Christians to do the same. When Christians perpetrate violence in the name of Jesus as in the historic examples of the Crusades and the Spanish Inquisition, we bring open shame to the name above all names, and we give our great enemy room to point his finger and say, "See there! I told you! They are a bunch of hypocrites after all."

I can't tell you the number of people who have cited the Crusades to me as one of the reasons why they do not believe in Jesus Christ almost 1,000 years after the fact. Christian violence and oppression shatters the witness of true believers and is a very difficult obstacle for outsiders to overcome.

Angelic Visitation

The power of the spirit of religion is that it completely blinds our eyes to the error of our ways. From slaughtering and enslaving Native Americans to intimidating Black Americans with nooses and burning crosses to colorblind laws that look good on paper but actually perpetuate oppression, we have allowed our religious devotion to hinder us from recognizing and repenting of our shameful mistreatment of the very least in our society. It's one thing to violently oppress another human being or an entire people group. It's a whole different thing to do it under the banner of Jesus Christ.

One of the clearest and most shocking examples of this disconnect is the fact that lynchings during the Jim Crow era were frequently held after church on Sunday afternoons and attended by White churchgoers (to include women and children) who proudly stood around the corpse for photographs, which were later distributed publicly as post cards. The phenomenon of the Sunday lynch mob clearly demonstrates the depth of the psychological and theological stronghold that the spirit of religion had on White church culture.

Jesus said that those who are well have no need of a physician, but rather those who are sick (Mark 2:17). Sadly, the spirit of religion has prevented sick people in the American church, from our earliest days until now, from identifying our spiritual malady and seeking a remedy. It has caused us to focus on tithing "mint and dill and cumin" while simultaneously neglecting "justice and mercy and faithfulness" (Matthew 23:23). It has made us to resemble "whitewashed tombs, which outwardly appear beautiful, but within are full of dead people's bones and all uncleanness. So you also outwardly appear righteous to others, but within you are full of hypocrisy and lawlessness" (Matthew 23:27-28).

One of the functions of the church is to expose the sin that any particular culture is most vulnerable to, in order to help people avoid falling into the traps of the enemy. Yet rather than bucking up against and challenging the societal structure of the day, the status quo of oppressive race relations, the White church in America conformed complacently to it from the start and has actually functioned as one of its strongest advocates for hundreds of years.

The religious spirit has effectively paralyzed the American church from performing her primary function in society, which is to show the culture how to love one another regardless of race, ethnicity, gender or background. Rather than preaching the equality of all men and women in the sight of God, we have preached and perpetuated a cultural bias that has separated us as a nation for centuries and resulted in incredible suffering for millions upon millions of people.

Just as the church in Germany sat idly by as the Nazi regime rose to power and committed crimes against humanity against the Jews, the White church in the United States has allowed and even helped to perpetuate centuries of brutal oppression, all on our watch. Rather than focusing on our role as God's people to fight for justice and to speak out against evil, our focus has been on church attendance and religious activity.

Because the displacement of Native Americans and the enslavement of Africans were both so prosperous economically, we as a nation desired and chose wealth over morals. And unfortunately even the church found a way to justify our decision. The social pressures of the day drove the theology of the White church rather than vice versa, and the foundation of our entire nation is still suffering for it to this day.

Rather than walking in God's great commandment of love, we partnered with a theology of compromise to justify our greed. As a result, we missed the mark of love that God was setting for us as a budding nation. And as time went on, the eyes of people in America and all over the world began to be opened to the fact that our social structure and racist theology could not stand.

A major course correction was needed—in fact, two course corrections. How different American history could have been (and how many lives could have been spared) if the White church had been on the forefront of the fight for Emancipation and Civil Rights rather than coming around reluctantly on the tail end?

Greed

THE AREA OF LAND we know today as the continental United States of America is so vast and so unique, just as a landmass, it is impossible to fathom the unlimited potential it represented to the first settlers who arrived here. Contrast landing on the east coast of America and having more than 2,500 miles of rich, uncharted territory stretching out before you versus landing in the Dominican Republic or Jamaica, both of which are smaller in total area than the state of Connecticut. Or even Australia, which is a huge landmass but covered mostly with vast swaths of uninhabitable desert.

America was destined for economic greatness from the very beginning. With England's resources and global dominance combined with the almost unfathomably rich natural resources represented here, the British colony in North America was set apart from all other European colonial hubs. The only problem is that we had two moral obstacles standing in our way. First, the land was already occupied. And second, who would work the seemingly endless amount of potential farm land?

I have often wondered whether I would have done anything different if I were in the shoes of the first American settlers or if I would have gone right along with the program just like everyone else. Either way, the fact of the matter is that greed undoubtedly crept into the American equation, and the culture as whole, which is only the sum of the individual parts, chose to partner with greed rather the gospel.

Slavery and oppression are both terrible examples of mankind's fallen human nature, and there is nothing new about them. But when these things are done under the banner of Jesus Christ, I believe it is one of the greatest insults to the Lord we can possibly perpetrate. The God who is love personified cannot be accurately represented in a system of oppression, and as a result, many are turned away from him when atrocities are committed in his name.

The combination of the spirit of greed, to build wealth regardless of the human and social cost, mixed with a spirit of religion, which hides our sin under the cover of religious devotion (beautiful worship services in beautiful churches), was a one-two punch to the budding soul of America. While feeling justified before God, this land became full of dead men's bones, literally.

In the 16th chapter of Ezekiel, the prophet shares an interesting and revealing insight about the downfall of Sodom and Gomorrah, exposing the true root of their wickedness as a culture. "Behold, this was the guilt of your sister Sodom: she and her daughters had pride, excess of food, and prosperous ease, but did not aid the poor and needy" (Ezekiel 16:49). We have all read the account of the destruction of Sodom and infer that their core sin was homosexuality, but it turns out that sexual perversion was merely a symptom of a much deeper root. The real underlying sin of Sodom, and the real underlying sin of America, is greed.

Jesus told a parable in Luke chapter 16 about a rich man who wore extravagant clothes and had a feast on his table every day. At the gate of his house, a beggar sat day by day wishing that he could only get some table scraps from the rich man's daily feast. He lived with the dogs who licked his sores and provided him a small degree of relief as the man passed him by day after day.

Angelic Visitation

The story goes that both the poor beggar and the rich man died and went on to the afterlife, the poor man to heaven and the rich man to hell. The rich man calls across the infinite divide for any manner of relief from the suffering he is in, yet all of his requests are denied. He is left to suffer eternally because he did not share the blessings he was given in this life with those around him. Although he was a Jew and most likely a religiously devout man, he missed heaven because he did not love his neighbor.

In much the same way, the pattern of Jesus' parable can be seen from the very start in America. Consider the layout of a Southern plantation. White landowners built large ornate houses for themselves while providing one room shacks at the very gates of those mansions for their slave laborers. They provided their slaves with barely enough food and clothes to survive while they themselves wore the finest clothes and ate the richest food available at that time.

Day after day, they passed by the poor slaves going in and out of their homes and neglecting the plight of real human beings who were crammed into tiny huts where the kitchen and the sleeping quarters were one and the same. The Black children often ran around naked and barefoot, while the White children paraded around in their Sunday best.

Amazingly, the same pattern of the plantation exists in the layout of cities all across America today. In Charleston, the elite South of Broad neighborhood boasts of towering, ornate mansions owned almost exclusively by Whites, yet one block north of Broad Street sits a project neighborhood consisting of squatty, dilapidated brick apartments inhabited almost exclusively by Blacks.

In order to get off the peninsula, you have to drive by the poor men and women who live proverbially at the very gates of the South of Broad community. They are given just enough rent, food and clothing to get by, with no extra frills like light bulbs and nine volt batteries. Growing up in Charleston, my family and I drove by these projects on a daily basis, yet not once did I stop and think about the men and women living in poverty right in my own backyard.

When people visit Charleston, they inevitably tour the quirky, often one-way streets zigzagging through South of Broad, admiring the large, beautiful homes and well-preserved historic architecture. They flock to the historic churches, which are even more ornate and pristine, towering over the cityscape with their steeples rising to the heavens.

Yet how many tourists who visit Charleston each year take a tour of the Eastside? How many go to the Jackson Street projects to see where Latoyah and her family live? How many tour guides mention the other half of the equation, the poor man at the gates of the rich man's dwelling? No, we let the dogs lick their sores. Out of sight is truly out of mind.

What scares me about Jesus' parable is its close parallel to the world I grew up in and the world I see around me to this day—and the countless souls who are unwittingly walking in the same exact path as the rich man to their eternal demise. Every Sunday, we leave our beautiful ornate homes to attend our beautiful ornate churches to enjoy our beautiful ornate services, only to find on the Day of Judgment that we completely missed God's heart of love for his hurting and broken children who are suffering at our very gates.

Pain is real, and the problem of pain is that it can't be ignored. Well, we do ignore it as long as it's someone else's pain. But the gospel doesn't give us this out. The reality is that we are our brother's keeper and that loving our neighbor as ourselves is a big deal to God. All of the fullness of the Lord's heart is fulfilled when we love.

Notice in the parable the only details given about the man who went to hell are, one, that he was rich and, two, that he neglected the poor. Nothing about his belief in God or his religious devotion is even mentioned. Just as the prophet Ezekiel described, he had "pride, excess of food, and prosperous ease, but did not aid the poor and needy." What more evidence did God need against him for a guilty verdict?

More than once in the gospels, Jesus explicitly links our salvation to our care for the poor, but never to our religious devotion. In the parable of the sheep and the goats, he separates all of humanity into two categories based on one simple criterion. Not whether people attended church or read their Bibles or prayed every day, but whether they took care of the "least of these" (Matthew 25:40).

Those who fed the hungry and gave drink to the thirsty and clothed the naked and housed the stranger and visited the sick and the prisoner are welcomed into the eternal Kingdom of God, while those who neglected the needs of their hurting neighbors are cast into hell. Yes, salvation is only gained by grace through faith, but faith without works is dead, and we cannot say we are saved Biblically unless our lives exhibit the works of mercy which Jesus shared through his teachings and his very life.

The Kingdom of God is an upside-down kingdom. While the world looks on great displays of wealth and ascetic beauty with awe and wonder, God sees things very differently. When God sees the Great Wall of China, does he rejoice over an architectural marvel or does he mourn over the million lives lost during its construction, most of whom were forced laborers? When God looks at the opulence and pristine beauty of the homes South of Broad, does he celebrate the charm of a well-preserved Southern American city or does he weep over generation after generation of slavery and oppression that built it?

God is really not that interested in the grandeur of our architecture or the vastness of our wealth—but he is relentlessly pursuing our hearts. And unfortunately we have elevated the former above the latter. I believe that it is time for a massive heart check in America. We have allowed the spirit of religion to convince us that we are right before God because we have checked all of the religious boxes, yet all the while, we have allowed greed to run rampant in our individual lives and corporately as a nation. We have "pride, excess of food, and prosperous ease," yet we step right over the poor man at our gates and neglect our very own Lord Jesus suffering in our streets without a place to lay his head.

People often think that Charleston is nicknamed the Holy City because of the number of church steeples that grace our skyline. Yet rather than justifying us, our steeples condemn us. Rather than pardoning us on the Day of Judgment, our beautiful historic architecture will accuse us. Because right in the midst of all the wealth and all the affluence and all the prestige, Latoyah, Destiny, Rashonda, Jacynta, Taliyah and Tamera sit right at our very gates, on the outside looking in, longing for a piece of the pie, just a small share in the American Dream.

There are hundreds of little boys and little girls just like them. While our kids are on a pipeline to college and career, they are on a much different pipeline—the boys on a pipeline to life in prison and the girls on a pipeline to life on welfare. Unless someone intervenes. Unless someone steps in. Unless someone breaks the historic cycles.

The day Charleston becomes the Holy City is the day we stop pursuing our own happiness and start pursuing theirs. The key to our redemption as a city and as an entire nation is sitting at our very gates. Their happiness is the pathway to our holiness.

The true tragedy of the American story is not the innocent blood shed on our soil—God will bring justice and take care of all of that—but rather how many people have gone the same way as the rich man in Jesus' parable down to the pits of hell while holding fast to the belief that their religious devotion will save their souls. What a rude awakening awaits many of them and many of us today!

We comfort ourselves when someone dies that they were "a good person" and that are going to "a better place." I have yet to go to a funeral service for "a bad person" who is "going to hell." Yet how many of our deceased relatives and friends are begging God just like the rich man did in the parable to come back and warn their loved ones of the eternal punishment awaiting those who neglect the poor?

It's one thing for us to apologize for the sins of our past that have led us to this place—to issue a well-crafted individual or corporate apology—but confession is only half of repentance. To repent is to change our entire way of life. Repentance is more than lip service. It is making a complete 180 degree turn.

Are we ready to confess our error of partnering with the religious spirit to cover our greed as a nation and to start working together to fix the damage that has been done? Are we ready to build homeless shelters instead of fellowship halls? Are we ready to renovate soup kitchens rather than our own kitchens? Are we ready to spend as much on our city's housing projects as we do on our own home repair projects? Are we ready to focus on devotion to the poor and needy rather than devotion to our church buildings and Sunday morning services?

The Lord spoke about the people of Israel in Isaiah's day, "they seek me daily and delight to know my ways, as if they were a nation that did righteousness and did not forsake the judgment of their God" (Isaiah 58:2). He saw their religious devotion and their fasting, yet he pointed them in a completely different direction, to a completely different kind of fast, just as he did for me over a decade ago on that dusty hill in Durham, NC.

"Is not this the fast that I choose: to loose the bonds of wickedness, to undo the straps of the yoke, to let the oppressed go free, and to break every yoke? Is it not to share your bread with the hungry and bring the homeless poor into your house; when you see the naked, to cover him and not to hide yourself from your own flesh?" (Isaiah 58:6-7).

The true call on the church, the people of God, is not to build more buildings or to hold more religious services, but to show the world love like it has never seen before. It is to care for the poor and the oppressed in the same way we care for ourselves and our own children. When we do this, when we follow God's fast, we will see the healing and restoration we have been looking for. "Then your light will break forth like the dawn, and your healing will quickly appear" (Isaiah 58:8, NIV).

We all want to heal the racial and political divides in our land. Yet we are fixated on all the symptoms rather than addressing the true root—our very own pride and greed. In the infamous words of Walt Kelly's Pogo, "We have met the enemy and he is us."

It turns out that we are the problem—but through Christ, we can become the solution.

CHAPTER FIVE

NEVER GONNA CHANGE

SHORTLY AFTER STARTING Kingdom Club, we launched a Bible study in the library of the girls' elementary school to give them an opportunity to include any of their friends who wanted to join us. With the separation of church and state, we were not sure what we were allowed to say and not say, but we were pleasantly surprised to discover that as an extracurricular program not sponsored by the school, we had the freedom to say or do anything we wanted, to include Bible study, worship and prayer in Jesus' name.

Week after week, we danced and worshipped together, we made crafts and played games together, and we taught the girls about the awesome love of God. We made giant posters with each of the nine fruits of the Spirit, and we went one by one through the character traits that define the culture of God's Kingdom.

After lining the girls up at the door to leave one afternoon, I instructed them to walk single file to the front door and to be quiet in case any teachers or administrators were still around doing their work. I opened the door, and without hesitation, three of the girls flew into the main hallway and began to run around shouting back and forth to one another.

I quickly followed them out of the door hollering at them to be quiet and noticed that one of the janitors had just finished waxing the floor. Before I had time to react, one of the girls got down on the floor and, much to my dismay, began doing pretend snow angels on the freshly waxed floor. I looked on with horror and amazement at the boldness of her disrespect, and as abruptly as she had started, she promptly jumped back to her feet and run out of the front door with the other girls. So much for the fruit of the Spirit.

My face turned beet red, and I looked to the janitor as a feeling of pure embarrassment crept my entire body. I attempted to apologize but found myself at a total loss for words. Before I could speak, he looked me straight in the eyes and said, "These girls are never going to change." I shrugged my shoulders and once again attempted an apology, but nothing intelligible came out. I wanted to get out of that building as quickly as I possibly could.

As I was driving home that afternoon, a thought came to me which captured my attention. Everyone in that school knew our girls, from the principal (who they unfortunately saw a lot of) to the teachers and even the janitors. Every one of them knew the challenge that lay ahead of us better than we knew it ourselves.

The girl who did the snow angel lived literally a stone's throw from the school in the project apartments directly across the street. Her older sister dropped out of school at 14 after having a baby, and to this day, she shares a room with her sister and her niece, who are now 18 and 4 years old respectively.

The one thing the girls seemed to know in their minds as undeniable fact when we first met them was that they were "bad" kids who lived in a "bad" neighborhood and who went to a "bad" school. When teachers and administrators, parents and neighbors talk openly about Title 1 schools and Section 8 housing, kids eventually catch on. Everyone knew—even the girls knew—that they were beyond redemption.

Yet I know that God can do anything. And I knew that this was a direct challenge from him. I heard his voice then, and it has resonated in my spirit since that day. "These girls can change, and they will change. Just stick with them, and I will do the rest."

The Kingdom Club had been given our divine mandate from the Lord—and ever since, we've had our eyes on the kids society says are "never gonna change."

Befo' Day Clean

Recently, my wife and I took our four children and the Kingdom Club girls to a performance by a dear friend (and former Kingdom Club volunteer), Ann Caldwell, who sings gospel spirituals with her acapella group, the Magnolia Singers. As we all sat around in a big circle with the rest of the audience, Ann and her team of incredibly talented vocalists recreated the atmosphere of the Praise House or the camp meetings where plantation slaves would congregate to worship the Lord.

With only a stick and a wooden box for instrumentation, Ann and her troop transported us back in time to a world we cannot even begin to imagine today. One of the most compelling songs, "Befo' Day Clean," explores how slaves would work tirelessly from sunup to sundown only to return to their slave quarters to attend to their own housework, which included gardening, hunting, cooking, laundry and anything else that needed to be done in order to survive. "Before day clean" means before sunrise the following day, which sheds light on how slaves were required to work night and day just to survive and to meet the requirements of daily life placed upon them by the cruel hand of fate they had been dealt.

During the presentation, Ann said something which struck a

chord in my heart. She said regarding the spirituals that "these were the songs of an unhappy people, contrary to what many think today." The slaves sang spirituals to cheer themselves up and for a brief moment to forget the bitter bondage of perpetual chattel slavery, a tortuous existence which ended only in escape, which was next to impossible, or death.

Her statement gripped me for two reasons. One, because of how true it was. It is easy to watch an acapella group singing spirituals and to forget the backbreaking labor with the hot Southern sun beating down on these tortured individuals long hard day after long hard day. But the second reason it struck me was because of the gross understatement I found her statement to be. Unhappy people are not what I think of when I think about American chattel slaves. These people lived in a literal hell on earth.

If you think I am exaggerating, all you need to do is to take a trip to Charleston in August and stand outside in the direct sun for five minutes. After that, drop a penny on the ground and stoop down to pick it up. Then repeat for the next 13 hours. Finally, come to terms with the reality that this is your life for the rest of your life and you will understand why I say they lived in hell.

I could make the same case for the Black community living under the oppressive and violent hand of Jim Crow. In many cases, the hours were just as long, the pay was just as bad, the threat of violence was just as real, and the hope for a better future for them or for their children was just as nonexistent. It was much like the tragic Greek figure, Tantalus, who was doomed for eternity to have refreshment dangled just beyond his grasp without ever being able to reach it. Jim Crow was a little slice of hell on earth for all who tasted its bitter flavor.

The biggest problem I have with performances like Ann's last night is that inevitably they wrap up the singing, and we all shake our heads and grieve a little in our spirits over what "the ancestors" (as she calls them) went through. Then we get in our cars, we drive to our homes, and we return to our normal everyday lives thinking, "Well, that was then and this is now."

But as we drove back to the Jackson Street projects on the Eastside of downtown Charleston, I could not agree for one minute with this thought. That now is much so much better and so much different than then. The most ironic part about the Civil Rights Movement is the twisted reality it has birthed in inner city America. Truly, the poor Black community has been propelled into a third dispensation of hell on earth, a literal drug war zone, and it lies completely under the radar of most of the White community and even parts of the affluent Black community.

On the way to church one Sunday morning, I asked Latoyah's mom causally what she thought about the War on Drugs, and she did not have a clue what I was talking about—despite the fact that she has lived her entire life smack dab in the middle of it. She grew up seeing young Black men violently taken from her community, placed in coffins and jail cells, and that is her normal. She has never known any other way of life. Yet she did not even know it had a name and worse, a political origin. Her own brother was up for life in prison for drug activity, but praise the Lord, their praying mother had a lot of faith. At the last minute, the judge intervened and had mercy. Today, he is a free man—although most assuredly an exception to the rule.

The enigma I have wrestled with ever since meeting these girls is what on earth happened between the Civil Rights Movement and today? How can we call the America we live in today a post-racial world? How can we even call Civil Rights a victory if this is what it has produced?

Income disparity, wealth disparity, housing segregation, school segregation and church segregation are all virtually as bad as they were 60 years ago, but now we have 2.3 million people, mostly Black and Brown, locked behind bars and living out the prime of their lives in six by eight foot cells, with another countless number of millions branded as felons and unable to reenter mainstream society.

The best way to experience the hell that inner city kids have been growing up in for the past 40 plus years is to listen to the historians who have chronicled it firsthand—rappers. I grew up listening to hip hop artists like Tupac and Master P on my way to private school rapping about gun fights and running from police helicopters, about selling drugs to buy food and hustling to survive, about hoping to end up in jail so they would have three meals a day and a place to lay their heads.

I thought it was all make-believe, an exaggerated caricature. But this was their life. Their real, everyday life. Being stopped and frisked on your way to school (whether you have drugs or not). Losing your best friend to gang violence or your brother to the criminal justice system. A mother longing to see her son. A son longing to see his mother. Spending your birthday locked behind cold metal bars. Hearing the echo of prison doors slamming shut on your hopes and dreams. A dad with a felony conviction wondering how he is going to support his son. A son counting the years until his dad's release date.

A Black friend of mine who grew up on the Eastside told me once that he has two shoeboxes under his bed full of newspaper clippings of obituaries of his childhood friends. Yet he has only been to two weddings in his entire life. We are nearly the same age, but the reality of our lives could not be further apart.

Then after years of research, I came across a missing link, a bridge between the hell of Jim Crow and the hell of the War on Drugs. It turns out that it's the same bridge between the hell of slavery and the hell of Jim Crow, only 100 years later—White resistance. And like the "Redeemers" who fought Reconstruction a century before, the resistance once again arose out of the White church.

THE MORAL MAJORITY

In 1979, almost exactly one decade after the signing of the last of the Civil Rights Bills, American evangelist Jerry Falwell Sr. and political activist Paul Weyrich started a political organization known as the Moral Majority. The main thrust of the organization was to rally evangelical Christians to vote for conservative political candidates who stood strong on certain moral issues such as promoting traditional family values, supporting prayer and Bible reading in public schools, opposing the Equal Rights Amendment, fighting the state recognition of homosexuality and banning abortion.

While many believe that the advent of legalized abortion and the 1971 *Roe v. Wade* decision was the catalyst for the formation of the Moral Majority, the case initially sparked very little political activism among evangelicals. It wasn't until the late 1970s that the Moral Majority movement found some real traction, around the most contentious issue of the day—school desegregation.

Although the Supreme Court ruled in 1954 with its *Brown v. Board of Education* decision that segregated public schools were unconstitutional, it wasn't until 1976 that they made a similar ruling about private schools, in *Runyon v. McCrary*. In the two decades between these two rulings, thousands of "segregation academies" were established with discriminatory enrollment policies to keep Black students from attending.

Sadly, the White church led the charge in communities all across the South in the creation and funding of segregation academies.

Although the United States had a long-standing tradition of Catholic schools, Protestant Christian schools were not predominant in America prior to the 1950s. A report commissioned in 1972 to analyze the progress of *Brown v. Board of Education* found that Charleston alone had 11 church-operated segregation academies, including my own alma mater.

Although the IRS technically gained the power to revoke tax-exempt status from segregation academies based on the 1971 Supreme Court ruling *Colt v. Green*, the enforcement of this policy proved difficult and was rarely exercised during the first half of the 1970s. Of the estimated 3,500 private schools that were formed following *Brown v. Board of Education*, only about 100 of them had their tax-exempt status revoked as a result of blatantly refusing to adopt even a nominal non-discrimination policy.

But when Bob Jones University lost its tax-exempt status due to discriminatory admissions practices in 1976 and the commissioner of the IRS proposed a more stringent enforcement of *Colt v. Green* in 1978, fierce backlash arose from the conservative Christian community. Fear of government interference into the sovereignty of church affairs, primarily in regards to church-run segregated private schools, became the catalyst for the groundswell movement which led to the official formation of the Moral Majority in 1979.

Paul Weyrich, who coined the term "Moral Majority" and co-founded the organization, later reflected on the origins of the movement:

> [W]hat galvanized the Christian community was not abortion, school prayer, or the ERA [Equal Rights Amendment]. I am living witness to that because I was trying to get those people interested in those issues and I utterly failed. What changed their minds was Jimmy Carter's intervention against the Christian

schools, trying to deny them tax-exempt status on the basis of so-called de facto segregation.

The Moral Majority was co-founded and spearheaded by Jerry Falwell Sr., a Southern Baptist pastor and the founder of Liberty University. Falwell adamantly opposed the Civil Rights Movement, stating that "[integration] will destroy our race eventually." In response to *Brown v. Board of Education*, Falwell said, "If Chief Justice Warren and his associates had known God's word and had desired to do the Lord's will, I am quite confident that the 1954 decision would never had been made. The facilities should be separate. When God has drawn a line of distinction, we should not attempt to cross that line."

Falwell fought against Martin Luther King Jr. and criticized the Civil Rights leader saying in 1965, "I must personally say that I do question the sincerity and nonviolent intentions of some civil rights leaders such as Dr. Martin Luther King, Jr., Mr. James Farmer, and others." In response to King's famous March on Selma, Falwell remarked that "preachers are not called to be politicians but to be soul winners." A decade later, Falwell changed his mind and jumped head first into the political realm.

The Moral Majority effectively galvanized White evangelical Christians into a cohesive voting bloc, and as a result of the organization's grassroots organizing and multi-million dollar media campaign, Republican candidate Ronald Reagan was elected president by a landslide in 1980, touted by evangelicals as a major victory for the moral direction of our nation.

But over the next eight years of his presidency, Reagan and his administration struck the deadliest blow to the African American community since Jim Crow by ramping up the War on Drugs and expanding the Prison Industrial Complex to a level that has made it practically irreversible—a shift which is still producing devastating effects to this day in poor Black America like radiation from a nuclear bomb.

The prison population more than doubled during Reagan's eight years as president, and 15 years after he left office, the US prison population had risen to 2.2 million inmates from around 340,000 when Nixon first declared the War on Drugs in 1971.

One would think that a radical rise in crime rates must be the culprit for such a dramatic increase in the incarceration rate, but there is no correlation. The rise of intrusive policing tactics and harsh mandatory sentencing laws initiated through the War on Drugs and subsequent Tough on Crime campaigns bear the lion's share of the responsibility. A dramatic shift in public policy, not crime rates, has resulted in the mass incarceration nightmare we have on our hands today.

It is estimated today that one third of African American males have a felony conviction on their record, nearly three times the level of 1980. The War on Drugs is devastating from many angles, but the reason it has been branded "The New Jim Crow" has more to do with the after-effects of incarceration.

Felons in our nation are deprived of many of the same basic rights that African Americans were stripped of during Jim Crow. In most states, they are not allowed to vote, receive government assistance, live in public housing, apply for financial aid or sit on a jury. Once again, a door was opened for African Americans to be legally and systematically discriminated against, no longer because they are Black, but because they are felons.

Yet perhaps even more tragic than the policy shifts ushered in by the Reagan administration, Ronald Reagan from his very first campaign speeches until the end of his tenure in the Oval Office resurrected one of the vilest and most soul damaging aspects of

Jim Crow—the vilification of African Americans and Blackness itself.

During Reagan's campaign for presidency, he spoke regularly of "welfare queens" who played the system to get more benefits than they were due. Without making a single explicit racial reference, his rhetoric made it very clear who he was talking about—African American women living on the dole. Just as Black women were depicted as ignorant, lazy mammies during Jim Crow, Reagan painted a new picture for our day and age of the lazy African American mother who refuses to work and who has baby after baby out of wedlock to get more government assistance.

Tragically, this image has persisted in the collective psyche of White America to this day, despite the fact that the majority of welfare recipients by sheer population numbers are White. The mothers and grown older sisters of the Kingdom Club girls work harder than most people I know, yet they are still often unable to make ends meet. Even with welfare assistance, it's nearly impossible to make a living these days working at or near the minimum wage.

In the same vein, Reagan and his administration launched a media campaign in the mid 1980s to raise public awareness for the "demon drug" of crack cocaine. These news stories were run on every national news outlet depicting dangerous drug criminals who were exploiting a community teeming with "crackheads" and "crack whores." Nearly all of the images were of African American males.

Just as cartoons of Jumpin' Jim Crow defined what it meant to be a Black male in America for nearly 100 years—a stupid, lazy buffoon who was aggressive toward White women—the new prevailing image of the Black male in America became that of the drug criminal. We all know the scene without even thinking, a young Black male wearing a hooded sweatshirt and baggy jeans standing on the street corner getting searched and cuffed and shoved into the back of a police cruiser. Menace to society removed, peace and safety restored to our streets.

The images flashed onto our television screens, they were printed in our daily newspapers, but even more, they became imprinted on our minds, the minds of young and old, rich and poor alike. They were even imprinted on the minds of the African American community, in many ways turning the community against itself. To this day, I can't see a young Black kid wearing a hooded sweatshirt without thinking in the back of my mind that he must be selling drugs.

It turns out that the suspicions I grew up with regarding the African American community were not an accident. Nor were they remotely new. In eight short years, Ronald Reagan brought back to life the two most harmful and devastating aspects of Jim Crow—legal discrimination and the vilification of Blackness itself—both of which have prevailed virtually untouched to this day.

After his death in 2004, Jerry Falwell wrote a commentary entitled, "Ronald Reagan, My Christian Hero," reminiscing that "He was as pro-life, pro-family, pro-national defense and pro-Israel—as we were." Yet is it surprising that nowhere on the "moral" agenda of the "majority" of Christians in the 1970s and 1980s is there mentioned a need to help the impoverished African American community—or just the poor in general?

Instead, White evangelical Christians all across the nation followed a self-avowed segregationist on a crusade to elect a President who opposed all of the major Civil Rights Acts of the 1960s, who resisted the end of apartheid in South Africa, who attacked affirmative action at every turn, who undermined the government's ability to enforce Civil Rights legislation, who cut government assistance to the working poor and who initiated massive tax-cuts for both the wealthiest Americans and corporations.

Ronald Reagan and Jerry Falwell both were products of their time, and Reagan's policies were more a reflection of the culture than the man. Blinded by the historic undercurrent of instructional racism, the Moral Majority movement reveals the same disconnect in the American church from our very first encounters with Native and African Americans. Deeply committed to "morality" and "traditional Christian values," we have missed God's greatest and most basic commandment to love.

Can you imagine how many abortions could have been prevented if the Moral Majority had rallied evangelical believers to care for the poor in our inner cities, to hold the hands of pregnant teens and single moms, walking them through the process of childbirth from start to finish—rather than picketing and protesting?

When Jerry Falwell closed the doors of the Moral Majority in 1989, he remarked that "our mission is accomplished." With more abortions in 1989 than a decade earlier when he began his crusade, I'm not sure what mission he was referring to. But I do know one thing—Falwell and his constituents repeated history in the worst way possible.

Almost exactly 100 years after White evangelicals rallied to help usher in the all-White Southern Democratic Party, the party that enacted and perpetuated Jim Crow for 75 years, White evangelicals rallied in support of an equally monochrome Republican Party, which employed the "Southern Strategy" to subtly appeal to racist sentiments in White voters across the nation—and who ushered in the era of "The New Jim Crow" we are living in today. Rather than championing the least in our midst, the White faith community once again found a way to oppose and vilify them.

And fast forward 40 years, we have a president in Donald Trump who is following Reagan's playbook almost to the tee—trickle-down economics, tax cuts for the wealthy, undermining workers rights, deregulation of industry, massive increases to the military budget while slashing domestic anti-poverty programs, the use of coded racial language and tough-on-crime rhetoric—and who continues to enjoy 75 to 80 percent of the White evangelical vote as a result. Their campaign slogans are even exactly the same, "Make America Great Again," a phrase coined by Reagan during his 1980 presidential campaign.

The Moral Majority movement has set in motion four decades of avid White evangelical Christian support of a new form of conservatism that has not only decimated the Black community, which has seen its median wealth fall by over one half in the past 40 years, but it has also gutted the American middle class. Between 1989 and 2018, the top one percent of Americans have seen their wealth increase by an astounding $23 trillion, while the bottom 50 percent have seen their wealth *decrease* by 900 billion.

Unwittingly, the modern Religious Right movement that has been birthed out of the Moral Majority has aligned itself against the interests of the working poor, both Black and White, and has embraced an economic agenda that has deepened the pockets of the corporate elite at the expense of the rest of Americans. That's not even to mention the full-on support of an ever-ballooning military budget and perpetual unjust warfare alongside harsh immigration policies which have been promoted through a new form of racist vilification of the Hispanic community.

Although we can see clearly in scripture that God's heart is for the poor, the oppressed and the marginalized, our racism has acted like blinders and led us into a whole new era of opposing the interests of the Black community, which is still the poorest demographic in our nation. And the evidence is clear. In the same 2016 election where 77 percent of White evangelical Christians voted for Donald Trump, only 3 percent of Black Christians voted for him, according to Pew Research. Now is the time for the White church to repent and realign ourselves with the heart of Jesus, whose stated purpose was to bring "good news to the poor" (Luke 4:18). He was rejected when he said it then, and I fear that we are continuing to reject him to this day by ignoring the heart cry of the Black community. This is our chance not to repeat history yet one more time, but to end up on the right side of history by fighting for the least in our midst.

THE NOISY MAJORITY

In 1969, in the wake of the Civil Rights Movement and in the midst of the Antiwar Movement opposing America's war in Vietnam, Richard Nixon called upon the "great silent majority" of American people to stand with him against those who were demonstrating in the streets. Although he used the phrase to highlight what he saw as the solution to America's most pressing problems, I believe he hit not upon the solution, but precisely upon the root of the problem itself.

When it comes to race relations in America, the problem is not the politicians. The problem is us. For nearly half a century, we the American people have stood idly by as the poorest and most vulnerable communities in our nation have been raped and pillaged by the War on Drugs in a way that is utterly unfathomable to anyone who has not experienced it firsthand. We have acted out Nixon's "silent majority" script in rare form.

When slavery ended, we silently tolerated Jim Crow. When segregation ended, we silently fled to the suburbs. When the War on Drugs was launched, we silently looked on as the New Jim Crow was born right underneath our noses. And since that time, we have silently watched our prison population rise to astronomical levels, both in sheer numbers and in racial disparity.

How much longer will we be silent? What will it take for us to raise our voices collectively and demand an end to the hell of the War on Drugs and the New Jim Crow? We are all to a degree the product of our environments. I'm afraid that as long as we say that the Drug War and the mass incarceration system are "never gonna change," the precious children of our inner cities are doomed to that same fate.

Of course, there are always those who escape. But in our present reality, they are by far the exceptions to the rule. The school to prison pipeline is not a myth, and it is not a statistic written in ink. It is written every day in human lives that are lost to a cruel and unusual punitive system. Who will raise a voice on behalf of these voiceless children? Who will break the silence to set them free from police occupation and the heavy Big Brother-like hand of the criminal justice system?

The majority has been silent long enough. Let us raise a collective voice and say, "No more!" Let us fight for these kids like they are our own. Because they are our own. We are all in this together, and no matter how you slice it or dice it, we all pay when children in our communities suffer.

Five years ago, I didn't know any of what I have written in this book. Regardless of where you are, whether this is the first time your eyes have been opened to the reality of racial disparity in America or whether you have been advocating for justice for decades, it's never too late to join the fight. We are the problem only up until the point when we decide that enough is enough—and then we can start to become the solution.

In 2015, Donald Trump resurrected the term "silent majority" while on the Presidential campaign trail. I believe we need just the opposite. America needs a "noisy majority" who will not tolerate injustice and evil, particularly when it targets the poorest of the poor.

We need an army who will "learn to do good; seek justice, correct oppression; bring justice to the fatherless, plead the widow's cause" (Isaiah 1:17).

God is able, but he needs willing vessels. Will you raise your voice with me?

Kingdom Club

After four years of walking through life with six unlikely friends from the Eastside of downtown Charleston, I wish that I could say all is well with them, that none of them are failing math, that they are all reading at or above grade level, that none of them are borderline truant because of their number of absences and tardies—but I would be lying if I did.

The reality is that even with more volunteers than we have students, our Kingdom Club journey is a daily struggle, and the problems we face are far above our scope. The War on Drugs continues to bring violence and intrusive police occupation into the girls' front yards. Welfare dependency continues to perpetuate a destructive mindset about life and what the future has to offer. The lack of wealth and resources in the community continues to stand as a barrier to the transition out of entitlement into empowerment. And there is no economic engine to lift the community out of its historic poverty.

It is often said that slavery and Jim Crow are past and that since the end of the Civil Rights Movement, the playing field has been leveled. But this line of reasoning falls dramatically short of reality. Black people emerged from the institution of slavery with very little education, fractured families from the constant sale of spouses and children, injured bodies from the abuses of slavery, social and emotional wounds from 250 years of bondage and rejection, and almost no land or property to build a future with.

They were then propelled into an era of social, political and economic oppression where any and all advancement was resisted both legally and illegally by fellow citizens as well as authorities of every kind. Fear plagued them at every turn knowing that if they did not step far enough off of the sidewalk or perform the societal dance of Jim Crow that they, and often their entire families, were at risk of violent retaliation, loss of employment, destruction of personal property or worse.

Our international War on Terror waged after 9/11 is ironic in light of the fact that we perpetrated a century-long regime of domestic terrorism against the Black community in the South. The awful power of terrorism does not lie in the few lives that are lost during any one particular attack, but the gripping fear that these displays of force leave in the hearts and minds of society at large.

Thousands of lives were lost on 9/11, but millions upon millions of lives are still affected each and every day by the cost, hassle and sheer embarrassment of the additional security measures enacted in its wake. In the same way, the thousands of lynchings and beatings, false accusations and imprisonments, employment abuses and firings that Black people faced as a result of noncompliance during Jim Crow cast a dark shroud of terror over the rest of the culture that literally paralyzed them and kept them in line.

Black mothers strictly warned and trained their children never to transgress the invisible boundaries of Jim Crow for fear of losing their babies. They walked a fine line themselves knowing that any perceived slight against a White person could and would invoke some form of retaliation. Black men had it the worst and could lose their livelihood or even their very lives for glancing too long in the wrong direction if a White woman happened to be in the line of sight.

But one of the most psychologically difficult aspects for White people to comprehend is that the authorities were often just as bad or worse than the perpetrators of violence (and often were the perpetrators of violence themselves) who threatened the lives of Black Americans. When a police officer stopped a White driver during Jim Crow, it may have been a nuisance, but when a police officer stopped a Black driver, it was a gripping ordeal. When someone cannot trust or turn to the civil authorities for personal protection, they are truly locked in a world of fear where there is no escape. Sadly, this is an aspect of Jim Crow that has carried over full force into our day.

For Black people, Jim Crow was a war zone, and just as many soldiers emerge from wartime encounters wrestling with post-traumatic stress, the same is most definitely true for the Black population in America, all over the nation but particularly in the South. The problem is that while our soldiers have resources and validation to help them overcome their condition, the Black community coming out of Jim Crow had neither.

So on top of the economic, educational, political and social setbacks that Black people faced following Jim Crow, there was an underlying current of psychological trauma that must be recognized if we are to understand the whole picture of our current landscape. The argument that the Civil Rights Movement completely leveled the playing field is beyond farfetched.

Can you imagine never once in your life being addressed as "sir" or "ma'am," "mister" or "misses", but every day having White people younger than you and even children address you derisively as "boy" or "girl" or just "nigger," commanding you to comply with their request to give up your seat or move off the sidewalk or some other whimsical demand designed to humiliate you? Only the elderly in the Black community escaped this moniker and were called "uncle" or "aunt," which was equally derogatory in its usage.

When someone is wounded repeatedly, again and again and again, the pain they experience eventually becomes internalized and makes it very difficult to trust anyone or anything that is connected to the source of that pain. The three and a half centuries of unreserved and unrestrained rejection simply cannot be wiped away overnight nor can it be glossed over now that we have at least publically admitted and repented of our grievous mistake.

I believe the biggest problem White people have with the entire conversation about race relation is that we have absolutely no way to experience or fully understand the painful depth of rejection that Black people have felt and continue to feel as a result of past and present prejudice against them. We can try as hard as we like to see the world through another person's lens, but we can never truly walk a mile in their shoes to know the magnitude of the hurt that they carry.

To be rejected as violently and vehemently as the Black community has been in the United States—from the Southeast all the way to the West Coast—for as long as they have from the mainstream social and economic order is a phenomenon that no outsider will ever be able to fully comprehend. You can tell someone all you want to "get over it," but the reality is that this depth of pain is not going away overnight, particularly because there are significant ramifications which are still persisting to this day in nearly every facet of our culture.

Even without the tragic compounding of the problem through White flight, globalization, the War on Drugs and the rise of the welfare state, we would still have our work cut out for us as a society. All of these factors combined have made matters exponentially worse and have perpetuated the trauma-filled environments that Black children are growing up in today.

I remember one day not too long ago when Nicole went to pick up the girls for some outing and she couldn't get to their apartment because the police had blocked off all of the roads. She finally got through and swooped up the girls to find out that someone had been murdered walking across "the cut," which is a little clearing right in front of the Jackson Street projects where the girls live. They not only heard the gunshots from their apartment, they knew everyone involved and the families of everyone involved, and as they were leaving the neighborhood, they saw the family of the murderer getting into two cars and speeding away.

As anyone who has ever visited a counselor knows, psychological trauma is very real and it does not disappear overnight. There is extensive research showing how trauma impairs cognition at the most basic level. The primary reason why none of our six girls are reading at grade level has less to do with the failure of our educational system and more to do with the trauma they are exposed to on a daily basis in their home environment. The reason why the Department of Education is failing our most underprivileged children starts long before they ever reach the schoolhouse.

The Black Church

WHILE I DO NOT BELIEVE that the Lord initiates or causes evil—that's the devil's job—I do know that He always find a way to use it for good. In fact, what is so awesome about God is how masterfully he uses the devil's own schemes, first and foremost the cross of Jesus Christ, to defeat him in the end. In the words of Joseph, "As for you, you meant evil against me, but God meant it for good" (Genesis 50:20).

The most incredible part of the Black narrative in America is not the harshness of the oppression or the magnitude of the greed that fueled it, but the unparalleled resilience of the Black community and the Black church in the midst of it all. If 350 years of brutal oppression and 50 years of marginalization can't break your spirit, then I suppose nothing can. In fact, just picture a Black church in your mind. If you're like me, the first word that comes to mind is "spirited."

Throughout all the long years of slavery and Jim Crow, the Black community had nowhere to turn but to the Lord. He was their "refuge and strength, a very present help in trouble" (Psalms 46:1). He was "[their] rock and [their] fortress and [their] deliverer" (Psalm 18:2). Just take a glance at any of the Psalms, particularly the ones that David wrote while on the run from Saul, and you can overlay them onto the Black American experience seamlessly.

God always sides with the oppressed. He "is near to the brokenhearted and saves the crushed in spirit" (Psalm 34:18). He "secures justice for the poor and upholds the cause of the needy" (Psalm 140:21). He "opposes the proud but gives grace to the humble" (James 4:6). When Jesus began his ministry, he declared that he had been anointed to preach good news, not to the rich but to the "poor," a word that can also be translated as humble, broken or afflicted.

The reason why God sides with the oppressed is simple—because they need him. The whole purpose of oppression is to dominate someone else and to render them powerless in order to exploit them. What the oppressed truly desire, deliverance from the hand of their oppressors, they have no ability to attain of their own accord. Otherwise they wouldn't be truly oppressed. So they must cry out to God just to have the most basic of human desires—freedom—fostering the dependence on God which lies at the very heart of the gospel.

Just as the Israelite slaves in Egypt cried out to God for deliverance for 400 years, the heart cry of the Black church since 1619 when the first African slaves landed on American soil has been for deliverance, freedom and justice. They may have been uneducated in the early years, but they were dialed into God's heartbeat "to proclaim liberty to the captives, and the opening of the prison to those who are bound" (Isaiah 61:1).

The sense of satisfaction and pride that the Declaration of Independence produced in White Americans simultaneously produced a sense of longing and yearning for a brighter day within the Black population. There is a desire in every human soul for liberty as described in the post-Civil War spiritual: "Oh, freedom, Oh, freedom / Oh freedom over me / And before I'd be a slave / I'd be buried in my grave / And go home to my Lord and be free."

In addition to siding with the oppressed, the Lord also gives them the gift of faith. My pastor at the time we started Kingdom Club, Brother Dallas, once told me that he had Black grand-mothers in his church with more faith in their pinky finger than I had in my entire body. Why? Because they needed their faith just to live and survive.

If you don't have enough money to buy food, you have to exercise your faith in a way that a person with a full pantry does not. You may both be Jesus-loving Christians, but the poor person is getting a spiritual workout while their wealthier counterpart is more at risk of becoming spiritually lazy. This is why Jesus taught us to pray for our "daily bread" (Matthew 6:11), to keep us completely reliant on God every moment of every day. The reason the Bible says that God has "chosen those who are poor in the eyes of the world to be rich in faith" (James 2:5) is not arbitrary—it's actually quite practical.

Since the oppression of the Black community has led to deep cycles of poverty over the past four centuries, Black people are statistically more vulnerable to poverty than Whites. Historically, this was the case in a way that we could not even possibly fathom today, but even half a century after the Civil Rights Movement, the wealth gap between Black and White is staggering.

According to a 2017 study by three Yale psychologists, for every $100 of wealth held by White families in America, Black families hold just $5.04. And for every $100 of income earned by White families, Black families earn $57.30 (yet our perception is that great progress has been made toward economic equality). As a result of this disparity, Black individuals and families are much more likely to experience poverty in their lifetime and therefore need to exercise faith for the basic necessities of life.

There are plenty of exceptions to this general trend, and it must be noted that more Black Americans have found success in the mainstream economy and culture today than ever before in the history of this nation. This should of course be celebrated, but at the same time, the middle and upper class Black community is not immune to the American trend of growing apathetic toward the poor. Wealth makes us comfortable, and comfort breeds apathy.

Thus, our call to repentance as Christians applies not only to the middle and upper class White communities, but to the middle and upper class Black communities as well. Jesus hardly ever addressed the issues of ethnicity and race, but he preached on money more than anything else aside from the Kingdom of God. The love of money is pulling both Black and White churches off course, and this is the representation of the church we often see on television and in the media. But the core of the Black church is alive and well, and we would all do well to learn from her vibrant spirit and unshakable faith.

When Brother Dallas and his wife arrived at St John's Chapel, the church on the Eastside we attended for several years, there was nothing but an old gutted community center with a toilet right in the middle of the floor. They prayed week after week in that ramshackle building with no resources, and God moved on their behalf. Everything in that entire church from the paint on the walls to the music coming out of the sound system is a direct result of faith.

Yet what amazes me even more than the soaring spirit and the inspiring faith of the Black church is the incredible grace and forgiveness they extend across the board, to White and Black, young and old, rich and poor. When my wife and I first walked into the doors of a Black church on the Eastside, we were welcomed with open arms and treated like royalty. And while this seemed perfectly normal to us at the time, neither of us really knew the history.

It would be easy for the people of St John's to have bitterness towards us considering our history as a nation, but in all the years we were there, we never felt the slightest tinge of resentment or unforgiveness. It is incredible to me how forgiveness and love flow so freely in the Black faith community, and there are no greater examples of this than following the tragic deaths of Walter Scott and the Emanuel Nine.

Although I do not want to discount the compassionate response of the White church to the Emanuel tragedy, it's the response of the Black church which is the miracle that traveled around the globe. The strength it took for the family members of the victims to look Dylan Roof straight in the eyes and to forgive him, one after another after another, just days after losing their loved ones reminds me of Corrie Ten Boom's famous story of forgiving the Nazi concentration camp guard. Because it wasn't just hate they were facing in that court room—it was layer upon layer and generation upon generation of pure and utter abhorrence. And yet there was no hint of bitterness to be found in their countenance or in their voices. That is the amazing power of grace and forgiveness in action.

Across the span of 400 long years, I see God's sovereign hand at work in molding and shaping a group of people through unimaginable difficulty and trial by fire. To me, the Black church is one of the major silver linings and redemptive purposes of American history. As I look at the landscape of the White church slipping more and more into self-help and prosperity gospels, I see the Black church with roots that have been developed over centuries of brutal oppression standing firm in the true gospel. I'm not talking about a building or a Sunday service, but the people of God living out the authentic gospel in the community day after day after day.

It is interesting that in the early days of American history, both the White church and the Black church indentified themselves with the children of Israel crossing the Red Sea and being delivered out of the hand of Egyptian bondage and oppression. Negro spirituals such as "Go Down Moses" and "Wade in the Water" express the longing for freedom held deep within the heart of every Black slave, songs which remained popular throughout the long dark era of Jim Crow and even to this day.

Yet where the roots of the White church were tainted from the bitter start by her alignment with British colonialism—both its utter disdain for and violent oppression of Indigenous people (not just in North America, but in Africa, India and Australia)—the Black church was birthed out an authentic heart cry for deliverance and salvation.

Where the White church has fallen into alignment time and time again with the agenda of the oppressor, the Black church has remained unwaveringly sided with the struggle of the oppressed, the marginalized and the poor. And as a result, the Black church carries a pure seed of the gospel that I believe has the potential to act as an antidote against the corruption and distortion of self-centered and self-serving Christianity.

There has never been a time in our history when we as a nation needed what the Black church has more than right now.

The Divided Church

The interesting thing about the racial divide in the American church (or any church for that matter) is how the New Testament does not make any racial distinctions whatsoever. We are taught that there is no Jew, no Greek, no Black, no White, no Hispanic, no Asian, no anything—just one body consisting of all Christians with one head, Jesus Christ. So for our congregations to be divided by skin color, as they have been for centuries and are to this day, is a glaring red flag that we are not alright as the body of Christ.

It's one thing for the world to be divided by race. In fact, the world will always be divided by race and self-segregate by ethnicity because the world focuses on the outward appearance of things. It feels comfortable to be around people who look, sound, act, dress and even eat alike. But these cultural markers, as powerful as they may be, are no match for the love of God. The love of God in Christ is unconditional, which means that we are called to love each other regardless of race, ethnicity, culture and personal preference.

Jesus died on the cross for every tribe and tongue, every nation and people group on the earth. His love crosses all earthly boundaries, and our love must do the same. Divisions based on outward appearance are not acceptable in the church because in God's eyes, they simply don't exist. The body of Christ is one whether we act like it or not. Like a house full of siblings, we will do a whole lot better if we decide to get along and work together. As Jesus put it, a house divided cannot stand.

The church is called to be the head and not the tail, the forerunners in our culture of demonstrating the love of God to the people around us. If the church can't show the world a model of unity, how do we expect our culture to bridge a racial divide that is centuries old and cemented into the very foundation of our culture?

Before we can come together as a united body, an undivided church, we must learn to honor one another and recognize the individual strengths that we each bring to the table. Our tendency is to always focus on the negative, the areas where other churches or denominations are lacking, rather than the areas where they are excelling. But if we focus on what the other has to offer, we can both be strengthened by our unification.

The White church needs the Black church to help us return to a Biblical cry for salvation, a dependence on God for all things, and an awareness of our need for social justice and mercy ministry. The Black church needs the White church for resources to build economic infrastructure in poor communities of color and to overturn oppressive government policies that are perpetuating cycles of poverty in these communities. And we both need each other for forgiveness, reconciliation and redemption.

Although we have formally forgiven one another in word and on paper, there is a deeper level of forgiveness that needs to flow between the faith communities of White and Black in the South and all across the nation. Otherwise, our churches would not be just as segregated as they were more than 50 years ago. Whether we like it or not, our lives and our salvation are integrally connected—Black, White and every shade in between.

In Jesus' last recorded prayer before he was arrested and crucified, he cried out to God for the unity of his followers, imploring his Heavenly Father "that they may be one, even as we are one" (John 17:11). Then he went on to pray for everyone who would believe after them, "for those who will believe in me through their word," which includes all of the saints who are in Christ down to this day, "that they may all be one" (John 17:20-21). And then Jesus makes a very telling statement. He reveals the ultimate purpose of his prayer for unity, "so that the world may believe that you have sent me" (John 17:21).

If unity causes the world to believe, then what is our disunity doing? Jesus knew 2,000 years ago that when the world sees true unconditional love which embraces people across cultural, racial, ethnic, social, political, economic and geographic divides that it will be a witness for his deity beyond any argument or apologetic we could ever speak.

All of our churches are strategizing right now about how to get Millennials through the doors. But when we become unified as the true body of Christ—Black and White, Hispanic and Asian—Millennials will flock to us. They will be knocking down our doors because they are the social justice generation, and they are dying for an answer. They are dying to know the truth. They are dying to experience a love that knows no bounds.

This is why Jesus died, to give his love to them. The question is, are we willing to follow his lead?

THE UNITY MOVEMENT

THE REAL DIFFICULTY of a book like this is finding where the rubber actually meets the road. What do we do in response to all of this? When the Civil Rights Movement of the 1950s and 60s was reaching its climax, the battle lines were clearly drawn and everyone knew the objective—to tear down Jim Crow and to end legalized racial segregation in America. More than half a century later, the battle lines aren't so clear. Government mandated segregation is nothing more than a distant memory, yet it feels at times like racial tension is going to tear us apart at the seams.

Although I don't believe anyone can predict what the unity movement that is hidden in God's heart is going to look like, I have two core convictions about where to go from here, neither of which will likely make me very popular among my White peers.

First, I believe that the next move in the chess match of racial reconciliation belongs to the White church, and second, I believe that it must involve monetary reparation. Martin Luther King, Jr. remarked in 1965 that his greatest miscalculation throughout the entire Civil Rights struggle was the response of the White church. He had originally thought that once the evils of Jim Crow were exposed for all to see and his White brothers and sisters in Christ witnessed firsthand the suffering of the Black community that they would vehemently rally behind him and his cause. Instead, they opposed him at every turn.

"[T]he most pervasive mistake I have made was in believing that because our cause was just, we could be sure that the White ministers of the South, once their Christian consciences were challenged, would rise to our aid. I felt that White ministers would take our cause to the White power structure. I ended up, of course, chastened and disillusioned. As our movement unfolded, and direct appeals were made to White ministers, most folded their hands—and some even took stands against us."

Even with the handwriting on the wall, many White Christians around the country and the vast majority of White Christians in the South continued to resist the hand and the voice of God as the Civil Rights Movement reached its climax. Rather than partnering with the Black community's cry for justice and equality, the White faith community openly opposed the movement, effectively turning its back on the suffering, violent oppression and extreme poverty of its Black and Brown brothers and sisters.

This resistance was pervasive among lay people in the church and did not come from the pulpit only. In fact, Southern church leaders who spoke out against Jim Crow in favor of Civil Rights faced strong backlash and were often forcibly removed from church leadership. While this is no excuse for not speaking up and speaking out, it demonstrates the iron grip that the stronghold of racism had on the culture of the White church all across the South.

Just as the religious elite of our Lord Jesus' day fought him tooth and nail every step of his ministry, White church leaders battled against King and other Civil Rights leaders until the bitter end of the movement and beyond as entire church congregations fled the urban landscape to the suburbs in White flight. When resistance to Civil Rights did not work, abandonment became the overall response of the White faith community.

A Black friend who works in inner city ministry with a focus on racial reconciliation told me recently that from his experience, most Black churches have moved on from talking about racial reconciliation while White churches are still hung up on it. When I asked him why, he explained that amid all of the talk, nothing significant has changed. As a result, Black churches have shifted their energy to addressing the practical needs of their communities and just keeping the lights on.

Like an extended right hand, the Black faith community put themselves out toward the White faith community during Civil Rights, and that plea for assistance and fellowship was vehemently denied. And although practically every White church in the nation has published an official "I'm sorry" statement, the next move toward racial reconciliation belongs to the White church. Saying sorry is only half of repentance. Repentance is to ask forgiveness and then to do what it takes to make things right.

My White brothers and sisters, the next move is ours to make.

REPARATIONS

MY SECOND CORE CONVICTION is that the move which the White church must take, whatever it looks like, must have an economic component to it.

When John the Baptist was asked by the crowds what they should do in response to his message of repentance, he gave three responses, all of which were economic in nature. He told the people to share their extra clothes and food with the poor, he told the tax collectors to stop padding their income through deceit, and he told the soldiers to stop extorting money and to be satisfied with their wages (Luke 3:10-14).

When the rich young ruler came to Jesus asking about eternal life, Jesus did not lead him in a sinner's prayer (as most of us evangelists would have done in a heartbeat). Instead, he told the man to sell all that he had and give the money to the poor (Mark 10:17-27). When Zacchaeus encountered the love of God through Jesus' spontaneous visit to his house, his repentance to God was purely economic. He pledged to give away half of his money to the poor and to give four times to anyone whom he had defrauded (Luke 19:1-10). If that's not reparations, I don't know what is.

I realize that simply by uttering the word "reparations," I am entering a heated political debate which many feel passionately about. I can already feel the temperature in the room rising. However, when we take a step back from the sociopolitical dynamic, the concept of reparations is one that every single person on the planet understands intuitively.

If I run into your fence with my car, someone has to cover the cost to repair the damage that was done. Economic reparations are fundamental to reaching true justice in any case involving injury or property damage, and the billboards that line our interstates advertising for injury lawyer after injury lawyer only testify that our culture has no problem at all understanding the concept.

Additionally, there is an example from our own history which I believe has the potential to shed some light for us on the entire reparations debate. Between 1988 and 1998, the United States federal government distributed $1.6 billion in reparations to nearly 82,000 Japanese Americans who were forcibly removed from their homes in the Spring of 1942 (due to racial hysteria at the outset of World War II) and held in internment camps until January 1945, after the US Supreme Court declared their detention unconstitutional. Each surviving detainee received a financial redress of $20,000.

Although brief, this period in our nation's history is a shocking and sad example of how racial prejudice mixed with enough propaganda can destroy the fabric of our communities and cause incredible human suffering. Without going into too much detail, the process from start to finish of these Japanese Americans (most of whom were United States citizens) was utterly tragic—forced from their homes with only what possessions they could physically carry, imprisoned in deplorable conditions for three years and then released back into their communities with only a $25 train ticket and nothing to rebuild with. The majority lost everything they owned and faced incredible discrimination in the process generated by the frenzied media campaigns, which history has revealed had no basis in reality.

While I believe the redress in this particular case was necessary and appropriate, it does provide an interesting perspective on the reparations debate regarding Black Americans emerging from the periods of slavery and Jim Crow. These Japanese Americans who suffered three years of hardship and property loss were rewarded a substantial redress, and rightly so. But what about the 350 years of hardship and property loss endured by the Black community? And the past 40 years of a devastating, politically motivated drug war? If we can agree that a financial settlement was the moral and expedient response to the injustice done to Japanese Americans, can we not agree that the same is due for African Americans, whose length and depth of suffering is completely incomparable?

The interesting thing is that the "Redress Movement," started by a younger generation of Japanese Americans to obtain an official apology and reparations from the federal government for the horrible injustice done to their grandparents' generation, was inspired by the Civil Rights Movement. And ironically, it was signed into law by Ronald Reagan in 1988 at the very same time Black Americans were being swept by the hundreds of thousands into the mass incarceration system through the War on Drugs he had ramped up just a few years prior. And the reparation awarded, $20,000 per surviving detainee, is greater than the net worth of the majority of Black families living in America today.

Clearly with a Black population in America of more than 47 million, government reparations for slavery and Jim Crow would be infinitely harder to implement and fund, but we can't let that stop us from agreeing that redress is due. The problem with our current reparations debate is that we have not even come to this baseline consensus. We have grappled with the questions of "how" and "what" without ever settling the underlying questions of "if" and "why."

Some people consider welfare a form of reparation, but the reality is that the two are night and day. Means-tested welfare is awarded to those who can prove their lack of income or wealth, and over time it actually discourages wealth building because it disincentives both income-generation and savings. Conversely, a lump sum of capital given at one time, as in the case of redress, encourages investment and could be used, for example, as seed money for a small business or as the down payment for a house, both of which are catalysts for further wealth creation.

Someone a whole lot smarter than me is going to have to figure out how to approach the reparations question, but it does not take a rocket scientist to see that redress for slavery and Jim Crow (and even the government's role in facilitating the post-Civil Rights injustices such as the War on Drugs) is long overdue. The fact that our Hispanic population, which started booming in the 1950s and 60s, is enjoying a greater slice of the American pie than our Black population, who have been here laying the foundation of this nation for four centuries, is a tragic shame. And none of us should be okay with it.

In addition to government reparations, I believe that the White church is culpable as well and that we must begin to seriously consider what redress looks like from our perspective. I think that one of the biggest mistakes the church in America made in the 20th Century was to let the government take the forefront in social issues, primarily caring for the poor. If the White church had responded to the cries of the Black community during Civil Rights (or better yet during Reconstruction), I don't believe we would have the mess that we have on our hands today.

Rather than appealing to the government for a solution, I believe that the White church has a responsibility to step up to the plate and make a concerted effort to repair the damage we have caused as a result of championing both slavery and segregation. The cost to the Black community of our theological position supporting these institutions (rather than challenging them) is incalculable. The redress and reparations that I long to see can't be mandated by law. I believe it must flow freely from the heart—out of God's heart through his people—if it is to have the intended consequence of bridging the historic race gap in American Christianity and the culture at large.

Clearly from the examples of Zacchaeus and the Rich Young Ruler, there are times when words or an apology or a prayer are simply not enough. There must be action taken in order to make amends. And look at Jesus' response to Zacchaeus' act of economic repentance. Immediately after pledging to give half of his net worth to the poor, Jesus said to him, "Today salvation has come to this house" (Luke 19:9). Zacchaeus did not pray a prayer or accept Jesus into his heart. He did not profess belief of any kind in God or Jesus. But his actions spoke louder than any words or even prayer ever could.

I believe the response of the White church to our violent opposition of both the Emancipation Movement and the Civil Rights Movement has been far too little and way too late. It took until 1995 for the Southern Baptist church to renounce their support of slavery and segregation. The Episcopal Church made a resolution in 2006 and gathered in 2008 to formally apologize.

By that time, the damage to the Black community from White flight, globalization, welfare dependency and the War on Drugs had already been done. What took the White church 30 to 40 years to make up our minds regarding the morality of slavery and segregation? And what makes us think that we can just say sorry and move on?

Can you imagine if cigarette companies had approached the lawyers behind the class action lawsuits of the late 1990s and said, "We're ready to settle this matter once and for all—we made a big mistake and hurt a lot of people, and we are really sorry"? I can assure you that a verbal apology is not what the lawyers were after. In fact, there was a kid who went to my high school whose dad drove a Lamborghini because those cigarette companies were forced to do more—a whole lot more—than just say sorry.

Despite the White community's disdain for reparations conceptually, it is interesting to note that the natural and spontaneous response to the Emanuel AME shooting from the local as well as the national community came in the form of a sizeable economic reparation.

I believe the outpouring of love and support toward the families of Emanuel Nine would have felt quite empty without a monetary aspect. It's one thing to hold hands across the bridge and to stand together for a couple of hours, but it is a whole different story to recognize and shoulder each other's financial burdens within the community on an ongoing basis, particularly when those burdens are a result of historic oppression.

THE WEALTH GAP

THE FUNDS THAT POURED into Mother Emanuel raise the question of the uncompensated losses which were common, everyday occurrences during the periods of slavery and Jim Crow. Black church bombings and burnings happened on a weekly basis during the height of the Civil Rights battle. Black homes and businesses were regularly vandalized, burglarized and burned to the ground all throughout the era of Jim Crow, and thousands of innocent Black men and women were injured or lost their lives in order to keep the social and political order intact.

You wouldn't even have to dredge up the abuses of chattel slavery to come up with a pretty decent case for reparations, but if you did, the scales of justice would be tipped even more starkly. Yet in light of the unimaginable injury side of the case for historic reparations, I believe the economic exclusions of slavery and Jim Crow rival any other aspect of the injustice that was perpetrated.

The whole reason why slaves were abused, beaten and killed during the pre-Civil War period, and why Blacks in the South faced violence, intimidation and death during Jim Crow was to oppress the entire people group both economically and politically.

Violence itself was never the root, but rather it served the purpose of keeping a system of free and later cheap labor in place for the growth of the overall economic system. During slavery, harsh slave codes were enacted to prevent slaves from running away or starting a rebellion by threatening draconian penalties for anyone who was caught. Fear is what kept slaves on the plantations, not fences or chains.

On the worksite, slaves lived under constant threat of the whip to keep them on task. Since escape was such a risky endeavor, most slaves resisted their bondage through small acts of sabotage such as slowing down their pace, feigning illness, pretending not to understand commands or destroying crops, tools or other property. As a result, violence and intimidation were the primary tools employed to keep slaves working hard and long hours.

Later during Jim Crow, public lynchings and other forms of violent intimidation were used to maintain adherence to the social, political and economic order. The threat of violence and retaliation were what motivated Blacks to endure the painful rituals of stepping off the sidewalk for Whites to pass by, moving to the back of the bus when Whites would get on, using the kitchen entrance at restaurants and being restricted to the "Colored" areas publicly posted all across every city and town. It is what kept Black workers, both domestically and in the fields, submissive to their often abusive employers despite the dreadfully low compensation they received.

So rather than focusing on the violence and intimidation itself, the real tragedy is the loss of economic opportunity created and sustained by the system of oppression. For 250 years in the colonies and later the United States, it was nearly impossible for Black people to build or maintain any wealth whatsoever. Then for the next 100 years, although more opportunity opened up, it was intentionally and ruthlessly suppressed at every turn.

And when all was said and done, the White community apologized and moved on, taking 350 years worth of accumulated assets with us. We moved to suburbs and gated communities, we transitioned our children into private schools, we shifted our labor jobs overseas and we never even missed a beat.

All the while, we have trouble figuring out why the poor Black community can't pull themselves up by their bootstraps and escape the evils of welfare dependency and drug trafficking that swept into their impoverished inner city neighborhoods created by White flight in the South and redlining (in response to the Great Migration) in the Northeast, Midwest and Pacific West.

It's easy to get distracted by the Black middle class, the fact that we elected a Black president, and the increased Black representation in popular media (particularly marketing campaigns). Many Black individuals and families have been able to rise out of oppression and find success in American culture. There was a small handful who managed to do it during slavery, there was a greater portion who found a way during Jim Crow, and there is an even greater portion of the Black community who are living out the American dream today.

But there are still massive pockets of historic Black poverty that have yet to be touched by the sweeping successes of modern mainstream America. Even the wealth of the Black middle class, those who have emerged from generations of poverty and oppression, doesn't begin to compare to the wealth of the White middle class.

Of course this applies to individuals and families, but it is amplified even more when we consider the wealth of our relationships and networks. If the average White family in America, which statistically owns 10 times more wealth than the average Black family, is connected to 10 other White families, then the disparity is multiplied exponentially.

If you are looking to buy a home, purchase a reliable car, start a business or go back to school, the likelihood that you will be able to move forward often depends on the affluence of your network. And due to the divided nature of our culture, these networks rarely cross the color barrier, meaning that the wealth isn't flowing across racial lines. We have come a long way, but it's not actually as long as many suppose.

One problem we face in properly assessing the situation is that we tend to focus on income rather than wealth. The dilemma with the poor is not that they have no income. Millions of Americans live on wage employment or welfare subsidies which provide them with sufficient income to make ends meet—when all is going well, that is. But the vast majority of these individuals and families own zero wealth, which insulates people from financial disaster.

When your car breaks down or your air conditioner goes out suddenly or someone gets sick or injured and there are no reserves available to meet the need, all it takes is one financial blow to cause the whole train to come off the tracks. This is why poor people move so frequently. They have a financial emergency or a budgeting slip that causes them to get behind on their rent, and they don't have any wealth cushion to help them get caught up.

While we don't actively recognize it, nearly every economic opportunity is created or enhanced by wealth. When you go to look for your first job, if you have a car at your disposal, the base of your search is automatically broadened and the extent of your opportunity enhanced. The same is true of access to appropriate clothing, equipment and tools, secondary education and even personal business connections, which are more prevalent among more affluent communities.

Wealth is what creates wealth, whether it be the capital and equipment needed to start or run a successful business, stocks and bonds invested in the market, real estate holdings that generate rent and increase in value over time, or even cash sitting in an interest-accruing back account. Without any wealth, our business opportunities are severely restricted. But with even a small amount of wealth leveraged correctly, the sky is the limit.

This is precisely why monetary reparations are so critical. By leveraging the wealth and the resources already at the disposal of the White church (the people, not the building), an entirely new economy could be created in historically impoverished Black communities. The only solution to welfare dependency on a large scale is entrepreneurship. And in order to have entrepreneurship, there must be capital investment (along with education and accountability).

In order to break the cycle of entitlement, where everything is given without any effort on behalf of the recipient, we must create systems that incentivize hard work and afford opportunities for ownership. If you don't own anything, you have nothing to lose. If you have no stake in something, you will never be fully committed to it. The very thing that has been denied to the Black community for 400 years—ownership—is the very thing that will break the generational cycles in that community.

Through the partnership of the Black and White faith communities, we could see much more than just unity in the body of Christ—we could see an economic revolution in inner city America.

Love Movement

In 1 Corinthians 13:3, Paul shares a timeless insight about giving: "If I give all I possess to the poor [...], but do not have love, I gain nothing." While the importance of opening our wallets cannot be overstated, if we do not open our hearts at the same time, our efforts will all be for naught. God is not after our money—He is after our hearts.

In light of this, the redress I'm calling for is a love movement that must originate in the church. Again, I'm not talking about a building or a service, but rather the people of God. Our first step is to simply stop and sit with the poor in our communities, to acknowledge in more than mere lip service the injustice that has been perpetrated and develop a strategy to actually redress the wrongs that have been done.

The power of Kingdom Club is not that we have figured out some global solution to the problem of inequity, but that we have stopped. We have stopped and listened and developed relationships that are allowing us to change the paradigm of the two disparate worlds in which we once lived. None of us are rich by Forbes' standards, but we have a whole lot more materially than those in the community where we are serving.

Because we are inherently sinful and selfish, human beings tend to think about giving in terms of what it will cost us in the natural realm, rather than what we will gain in the spiritual one. Jesus instructs us to store up treasure in heaven rather than on earth, and Proverbs tells us that when we give to the poor, we are actually lending to the Lord and that he will certainly pay us back.

The two worlds of rich and poor are integrally connected in God's economy. As one of the most basic tenets of morality, God expects those who have more than enough to share with those who lack the basic necessities of life. This pattern appears in both the Old Testament and the New. When the Israelites gathered manna in the wilderness, "whoever gathered much had nothing left over, and whoever gathered little had no lack" (Exodus 16:18). When the nation of Israel settled into the Promised Land, the Lord set up a year of Jubilee where all property returned to its original owner and all mortgage debts were canceled once every 50 years (Leviticus 25).

When Jesus was pressed on the basic definition of love and what it means to be a neighbor, he told a simple story about helping someone in need, about stopping and stooping and getting involved in someone else's pain and misfortune. Oh, and footing the bill when all is said and done. It's messy and costly to help a stranger in need. But morality at its most basic level calls for it, and there is no way to develop in God's love without incurring some form of personal cost.

As the wealthiest nation and lone superpower in the world, we have a responsibility and an opportunity to help the least in our midst, both locally and within the global community. Love is not rocket science. It's actually quite the opposite. It is following our gut reaction when we see someone who is suffering and in pain to stop and to help and to just do something. I'm sure the Good Samaritan felt ill equipped to help that bleeding man. He didn't have a Ph.D. in nursing. But he did have a donkey and some olive oil and a few bucks to pay for a hotel room. And above all, he had a heart.

Listen to the words of Timothy written to the first century church: "As for the rich in this present age, charge them not to be haughty, nor to set their hopes on the uncertainty of riches, but on God, who richly provides us with everything to enjoy. They are to do good, to be rich in good works, to be generous and ready to share, thus storing up treasure for themselves as a good foundation for the future, so that they may take hold of that which is truly life" (1 Timothy 6:17-19).

When we give, we have the opportunity to simultaneously alleviate suffering and to "take hold of that which is truly life." To give is to come alive. Not just here and now, but for eternity. I don't know about you, but I don't want to be rich. I want to be rich in good works. Because I know that every single time I have a chance to use my resources to alleviate human suffering, the kingdom of heaven is advanced just a little bit. And that is my heartbeat. "Repent for the kingdom of heaven is at hand" (Matthew 4:17).

My White brothers and sisters, let's meet the extended right hand of the Black faith community and let's do it with a generous love offering. Let us give of our time, our talent and our treasure and let's make things right between the Black church and the White church in

America. My prayer is that 50 years from now, there won't be a Black church or a White church or a Hispanic church in America—but only one glorious and united Bride of Christ.

Sound impossible? Perhaps. But nothing is impossible for Jesus.

Epilogue

Two days after we gave away the gold, my wife and I were invited to a ministry dinner hosted by a local non-profit that focused primarily on pursuing revival and fostering unity in the body of Christ. We had no idea who we would be seated with ahead of time but happened to be paired with a good friend who led worship on the closing night of the tent revival and her husband.

Before the dinner was served, we were all invited to join in a time of worship, so we each stood at our tables as the worship team began to play. As we were singing, our friend leaned over and starting telling us about an open vision she was having. She said that she saw gold coins floating over our heads, six coins total, of all different sizes hanging on white strings representing purity. She said they were absolutely beautiful.

Although I have never personally seen an open vision, I have enough prophetic friends to know that they are just part of life for some people. I know believers who have been getting visions since they were kids and others who have never seen one in a lifetime, but I know from scripture that God uses them from Genesis to Revelation, and I always pay attention when those around me have them.

Immediately, Nicole and I looked at each other and began to laugh out loud. We were stunned. We both had peace about giving away the gold, but it's hard not to let doubt creep into a situation where the step God asks you to take makes no sense in the natural realm—like giving away $80,000 worth of gold when you have three kids and no job.

Our friend went on to say that gold coins are the currency of heaven, that your life buys them, and that they are the most precious thing in all of heaven. She said that there was a real weightiness to the coins and that she could feel the weight of them.

I knew that this confirmation was God's mercy, and I instantly felt a release come over my entire being knowing that we were in the center of the Lord's will. His peace washed over me, and I knew in that moment everything was going to be alright.

Two months later, I got a phone call while driving with my family in the car. It was the same friend who had seen the gold coins over our heads at the ministry dinner. She started to share how the Lord had interrupted her prayer time that morning and spoke to her about Nicole and me.

"When you gave away the gold," she said slowly and intentionally, "a curse was broken off of your family. There was an open door for sickness over your family and now it has been closed because you were willing to give away your inheritance. It was dirty money, and a prayer of repentance would not have been enough. The Lord is giving you a better inheritance. Any more inheritance you receive from now on has been sanctified—you don't have to give it away too, just be wise with it. It will be an inheritance in the natural and in the spiritual."

In June of 2008, we discovered that my father had an inoperable brain tumor, and he died three months later. In September of that same year, my Uncle Preston found out that he had prostate cancer, and five months later in February of the following year, my other uncle, Charley, was diagnosed with lymphoma. Charley passed away in 2010 and Preston in 2016. In the span of eight months, all three of the males in my immediate family were diagnosed with cancer, all of which proved to be fatal.

We prayed and prayed and prayed for each of these men, they underwent treatment after treatment after treatment, yet nothing we did was able to stop the cruel hand of fate. I am not superstitious but I am well versed on generational curses, and here I am now with three boys of my own. To hear that this curse of sickness over my family was broken rang like unimaginable heavenly music to my ears. My wife and I immediately began to worship God in the car as the presence of the Lord once again washed over us.

It turns out that there are circumstances where verbal repentance is simply not enough. I don't begin to understand it all, but I do know that a certain freedom and blessing was released over our lives the day we gave away that gold—just like Zacchaeus. By paying recompense to those he had exploited in order to become wealthy, Zacchaeus was freed from his guilt both in his conscience and in the courts of heaven. And I believe there are many in our nation who are facing this same call from the Lord, to let go of their material wealth so that they can be set free in the Spirit.

When Jesus comes back, will the people of America be like the rich fool who built bigger barns in order to store up more treasure on earth? Or will we be like "the rich in this present age" who Paul implores "to do good, to be rich in good works, to be generous and ready to share, thus storing up treasure for themselves as a good foundation for the future, so that they may take hold of that which is truly life" (1 Timothy 6:17-19)?

This past year, we sent one of the Kingdom Club girls, Destiny, to a private Christian school where she came alive like never before. She played organized sports for the first time in her life, joining the volleyball team, the basketball team and the cheerleading squad. She was challenged academically, socially and spiritually, and she rose to the challenge in every area. She participated in project-based learning in cooperation with her peers, and although she struggled in some areas, she persevered through every difficulty. She even led worship for the very first time on stage for the entire school.

The tuition for the school year was $6,500, which we were able to raise by the grace of God, and we are well on our way to raising those same funds for this coming school year. But Destiny is only one girl, and we are going to need a lot more resources as the body of Christ if we are going to reach her generation and provide them with the opportunity that their parents and grandparents may have never had. I believe this is our time "to be rich in good works" and "to be generous and ready to share" (1 Timothy 6:18), not just for the sake of a tax write-off, but to empower a generation and to make right on hundreds of years of wrong.

Jesus himself is waiting for our response. For whatever we do for the least, we do for him. And whatever we do not do, well, the same applies. Both as a nation and as individuals. Now is our time. To reach out or to hold back. To give freely or to keep for ourselves. To be sheep or to be goats. And I don't know about you, but I know which side of that equation I want to be on. It's the side I want all of us to be on.

Brothers and sisters in Christ, will you join me there?

www.ingramcontent.com/pod-product-compliance
Lightning Source LLC
Chambersburg PA
CBHW031418290426
44110CB00011B/432